Endorsements

With candor and compassion, Kurt speaks to the core of societal mores, trends, and lies that weaken us. But he does better than reveal what's wrong with us and our culture. He arms us with bullet lists of "how-to" information for assessing our lifestyles, for avoiding the pitfalls of our human frailty, and for growing nearer the God who alone can transform us. Each reading ends with a suggestion for practical application and a ready prayer for the reader whose heart responds, "That's what I want and need."

Niki Anderson
Speaker and author of four award-winning books

In each devotional reading, Kurt Bubna sketches a brief and yet vivid snapshot—from the life of Jesus, from the experience of his own walk with the Lord, from the culture around us—and then gently urges us to see the deeper and broader picture, the truth that God would have us recognize. The warmth and wisdom that is found in these readings, drawn directly from the Word of God, encourages us to embrace the grace that God offers us, new every morning

Lorene Lambert
Ancient Egypt and Her Neighbors,
Who in the World is the Forgotten Explorer?

Pastor Kurt and Lindsay's collection of devotionals reflects real life and real struggles, but the authors don't wallow in those struggles. Instead, they offer a compassionate and biblically sound response. Readers will see themselves in this book and use it as a tool for growing in the strength of the Lord.

Ruth McHaney Danner
What I Learned from God While Quilting
and a regular contributor to *Open Windows*

No matter where you are at in your faith journey, this devotional is for you. We all have those days where we need that extra push, an encouragement, a specific word that speaks directly to where we are and what we are going through. All of us are human, our lives aren't perfect, the people around us don't do what we want, and our character constantly goes through the fire. The stories, verses and encouragement in this beautiful and honest devotional will resonate with your heart. Sit a moment. Soak it in. You will be glad you did.

Cami Bradley
Singer, songwriter and AGT finalist

We can only think of a handful of people that we know personally and professionally that we would jump at the opportunity to walk through their devotional life. Kurt Bubna is one of those people. *Perfectly Imperfect* is a practical, powerful and thought provoking resource to help men and women of any age navigate the everyday challenges and opportunities of daily life. We know Kurt to be grounded in the Word of God, candid, wise, encouraging and boldly vulnerable with his life experience. This book is a valuable tool to have for this mess of a thing we call life.

Mike and Lisa Fairburn
Founding Pastors, City Church Spokane

Perfectly Imperfect

A Devotional
for Grace-Filled Living

By Kurt W. Bubna
with Lindsay Branting

E Essential Life Press
vital resources for the christian life

Published by Essential Life Press (EssentialLifePress.org)
15303 E. Sprague Ave STE A
Spokane Valley, WA 99037

The stories in *Perfectly Imperfect* are true, but some names and
identifying details have been altered to protect the privacy of those
individuals.

ISBN-10: 0990902218
ISBN-13: 978-0-9909022-1-8

Dedication

To my mother, Virginia Faith Bubna-Mayo,
your devotion to Jesus, to your family,
and to me has helped me become the man I am.

CONTENTS

FOREWORD

They say that breakfast is the most important meal of the day. I believe them (whoever *they* are). So I rarely miss breakfast.

As much as my body needs breakfast, my soul needs devotions. I need to start my day by listening to God. We call it PBJ—shorthand for Prayer, Bible and Journal (not peanut butter and jelly). I read my Bible and ask God to speak to me, to give me one thing for the day. I write that one thing down in my journal, with an action step, and turn it into a prayer. This simple activity feeds and cleanses my soul, gives me direction for the day, and keeps me close to God.

Many have also found devotional guides, such as the one you hold in your hands, to be helpful. While I hope it doesn't replace your own daily engagement with Scripture, it can be very helpful to read what someone else's "one thing" is. It's like doing your devotions with a friend. It's PBJD ("D" for devotional)!

As you use this devotional, your new friends, Kurt Bubna and Lindsay Branting, will be sharing their "one thing" with you each day. They'll offer a verse or two of Scripture that spoke to them and pass on what it meant to them. And included with each devotion are practical suggestions for personal application and a prayer.

If I could pick any two friends to do devotions with, Kurt and Lindsay would be at the top of my list.

I've known Kurt since dinosaurs roamed the earth; we've been fellow pastors, backpacking and biking buddies, lunch partners and best friends.

I was there when Lindsay was born. I mean that literally! I was in the hospital room with her mom and dad only minutes after she arrived.

Besides my long and affectionate friendship with these two is the fact that both are gifted writers who love Jesus and the Scripture. And they've been doing PBJ for a long time, which makes them really good at the D part. Simply put...

They write great devotionals!

Don't take my word for it...read on!

Every day!

It will be good for your soul.

Joe Wittwer
Lead Pastor, Life Center
October, 2014

DAY 1: BECOMING GREAT

"You know that the rulers in this world lord it over their people, and officials flaunt their authority over those under them. But among you it will be different. Whoever wants to be a leader among you must be your servant, and whoever wants to be first among you must become your slave" Matthew 20:25-27 NLT.

Just about everybody wants to be great at something. Perhaps they want to be a great mom or dad, a great friend, a great skier or soccer player. There is something inside of us that longs for significance. I think God put that longing in our hearts.

So the question we must consider is: what makes a great man or woman great?

A while ago my wife, Laura, and I watched a very old movie. It was about Alexander the Great and starred Richard Burton (I told you it was old). Honestly, for my wife it was two hours and eighteen minutes of torture, but I loved it. I loved the history and the epicness of this story based on a ruler who lived about 300 years before Christ.

Alexander was an amazing conqueror, and he thought of himself as a god. He never lost a battle and ruled much of the known world at one time. He did all of this before he was thirty-two years old! During his final years, however, he exhibited signs of megalomania and paranoia. The sad reality is, Alexander was great by human standards, but not even close to being great by God's.

As I lay in bed that night after the movie, here's what I thought:

- True greatness is not measured by physical strength, but by the strength of our character.
- In the kingdom of God, greatness is not about conquering, but about serving.
- A great man or woman does not seek self-preservation, but selfless sacrifice.
- Great people are not known for their fickleness, but their faithfulness.
- By God's definition, greatness is all about love, not fear.

Our world likes to make heroes out of conquerors. God makes heroes out of the conquered. In fact, Jesus said, "If you want to find your life, lose it" (Mark 8:35).

I want to suggest that our God-given longing for greatness should be radically different from what we've been told in our culture. According to God, it is a path toward humble and selfless serving. True merit is seen in washing the feet of others and in dying to ourselves.

What next?

Be great today! Find a need and meet it. Willingly lay down your life for another. Serve like Jesus served.

May I pray for you?

God, you use different scales than we do to measure greatness. We want to exchange our scales for yours. Help us give sacrificially and serve others. Amen.

DAY 2: SUCCESSFUL RESOLUTIONS

"Commit to the Lord everything you do. Then your plans will succeed" Proverbs 16:3 NIRV.

A few years ago I resolved to lose 10-15 pounds before summer, but that was more like wishful thinking than a resolution. I hadn't determined a path to get from where I was to where I wanted and needed to be.

The result? I gained 6 pounds instead of losing 10-15. On the upside, there was more of me to love.

I believe in making resolutions. However, without a strategy and a resolve to carry it out, not much will get accomplished. Here's what an effective plan looks like:

- It has a clearly defined goal.
- It is stretching, but realistic.
- It has concrete steps, a defined pathway from A to Z.
- It has measurables that provide honest feedback regarding your growth and success along the way.
- It generally includes a support system.

Each of these five things is critical to your success. Without a goal—you'll wander. If it's too hard and unrealistic—you'll quit. If it doesn't involve clearly defined phases—you won't be able to celebrate the little successes along the journey. If there's no way to see if you're succeeding—you'll become discouraged because significant changes take time. And without the help of others—you'll probably slip back into old patterns.

Trust me. A plan matters.

There's one more important thing you need to consider: does your plan fit with God's plan? Over the years, I've learned that my potential for success is exponentially enhanced when I align my ideas with his.

What next?
When was the last time you made a resolution? You don't need to wait until New Year's Eve! Go for it!

May I pray for you?
God, we all have areas in our lives we'd like to grow and improve in. Show us those areas and then give us the wisdom, strength and perseverance to stick to a resolution for change! Amen.

DAY 3: ACHING

"You know what I long for, Lord; you hear my every sigh" Psalm 38:9 NLT.

There is nothing quite like the ache a parent or grandparent feels for their distressed little one. Whether the child is sick, wrestling with an emotional struggle or a physical challenge, our pain can feel overwhelming. It doesn't matter how old your kids or grandkids are, you ache when they ache, and you suffer when they suffer.

That's what love does.

I've wept over the struggles of those close to me. I would do anything to fix their situations. I've prayed over and over, "God, I beg you to intervene. Do something. Anything. Please come and fix this." At times the heavens seem silent.

But God feels every pain of every person in every moment of his or her life. Knowing the Lord is aware of our distress brings me comfort.

I have no idea what is causing you to ache in this moment. I don't know what brings angst and sorrow to your spirit.

But I do know this: God sees our troubles and cares deeply about the anguish of our souls (Ps. 31:7). He is near the brokenhearted (Ps. 34:18), and even when we walk through the valley of shadows he is close beside us (Ps. 23:4).

When life is hard, hang on to the truth, not what you feel. And understand this—God knows, he cares, and he is close.

What next?

Is your soul heavy right now? Lift your burden to the Lord and allow him to comfort you.

May I pray for you?

Father, this life is so hard sometimes. We don't control a great deal, and we feel overwhelmed by circumstances that baffle us. We know so little, and we ache so much. Please carry us. Please protect us. But most of all, please help us keep our eyes on you no matter what. You alone are our hope. Amen.

DAY 4: GETTING ALONG PART 1: CRITICS

"Love must be sincere. Bless those who persecute you; bless and do not curse. If your enemy is hungry, feed him; if he is thirsty, give him something to drink" Romans 12:9, 14, 20.

Many years ago I had a boss who hated me. To this day I don't know why (what's not to love?). She was an extremely critical person, and I rarely did anything right in her eyes.

Sadly, most of us have someone in our lives just like that. So how do you handle a person who constantly complains, is generally negative and critical, and often gives unwanted and mean-spirited advice? What do you do with relationships that seem to be more trouble than they're worth?

Here's what I'm learning about critics:

- Decide to love them no matter what. That may sound simplistic, but there is no greater force on the planet than the love of God shown through us. Our first and last response to our critic must be sincere love, and love involves blessing rather than cursing. We are able to love because God first loved us and empowers us to love one another.

- Endeavor to understand them. What's going on and how can you connect with them in the midst of it? For example, critics tend to believe that any task not in their hands will fail. They might not intend to be mean, but are often task-driven and motivated out of fear to avoid mistakes. All of this may be the result of personal insecurities cultivated by a parent they could never please. Take the time to stop, to think, and to pray about that critic in your life; it will help you to understand them better.
- Strive to listen to their words and their heart. Our tendency with a critic is to ignore what they say because of how they said it, but they may know or see something we don't. It's important to separate tone from substance. A wise person will accept truth and reject falsehood. So don't be proud, but instead cling to what is good. Tell them, "Thanks for pointing out those problems so that we can come up with solutions. What would you suggest we do?"
- It's okay to draw healthy boundaries. What if our critic is simply mean-spirited? Do we just become a doormat and learn to live with emotional abuse? Absolutely not. You can and should set reasonable and healthy boundaries.

Living with or working for a critic is tough, but be wise and view it as an opportunity to grow.

What next?
Today, be intentional about dealing with a critic in your life. Choose to love. Choose to grow.

May I pray for you?
Lord, sometimes it feels like we have more critics than friends. Help us discern truth from falsehood and to bless our enemies. Thank you for loving us unconditionally. Amen.

DAY 5: GETTING ALONG PART 2: CONTROL FREAKS

"Let us therefore make every effort to do what leads to peace and to mutual edification" Romans 14:19.

Once upon a time, in a far, far away place, I managed a telecommunications and customer support department for a bank. After just a couple of weeks on the job, I started to get anonymous notes and letters from several people in my department. They all said the same thing, "Our supervisor is driving us crazy by her obsessive, demanding, and controlling behavior."

I tried to work with the supervisor. I wanted to help her see and understand what she was doing, but I failed. She refused to change, and I ended up letting her go.

So how do you handle people who tend toward obsessive, demanding, and perfectionistic conduct? To begin with, it's helpful to understand the anatomy of a control freak. They are often driven by fear. They tend to be obsessive and bossy to the point of bullying, and are frequently perfectionists who become irritated easily.

So how do you cope with a control freak? Here's what I'm learning:

- Focus first on your character and their needs. This

relational principle is tough because most of us are inclined to do the opposite. We usually focus on *our needs* and *their character*. That doesn't mean we ignore their issues, but we start with our hearts first (Matthew 7:5).

- Pursue peace without compromising truth. Remember, in most cases a control freak's behavior is not a commentary about you as much as it is a strategy to deal with their own anxieties. Sometimes it's wise to "overlook an offense" and move on (Proverbs 19:11). Peace is, in many ways, the best antidote to fear and the best path to relational health.
- Consider the why and not just the what. Why are they controlling? One of the best ways to help them relax is to keep them informed. In fact, the more information a control freak has the better.
- Affirm and compliment them whenever you can. Try to focus on the good and encourage them.
- If a control freak continues to be obsessive, rigid, mean-spirited and unrealistic, then loving confrontation may be required, but be sure it is the truth spoken in love.

One last thing I want to leave you with: never underestimate the power of God and his love to transform people into his image.

What next?
Identify a control-freak in your life. Pray for change in them and you, and practice patience.

May I pray for you?
God, as far as it depends on us, help us to live at peace with difficult people in our lives. Amen.

DAY 6: GETTING ALONG PART 3: VOLCANOES

"A gentle answer turns away wrath, but a harsh word stirs up anger" Proverbs 15:1.

My dad was a volcano. He had an explosive temper and often lost it while driving our family car. One Sunday, my folks got into a nasty argument on our way to church. The madder my dad became the faster and more erratic he drove! The typical twenty-minute trip to church only took about ten minutes that Sunday.

What can you do with the person who is quick-tempered, explodes in anger, is unpredictable at times, and seems to have a chronic pattern of rage? Before we look at a few suggestions, let's consider some common characteristics of a volcano.

Volcanoes are emotionally unstable and can be rude, nasty, insulting and offensive. They are typically self-centered and generally believe the worst about people. They are easily upset by criticism because their own insecurities and guilt make them hypersensitive to any disapproval.

How do you handle a volcano? Here's what I'm learning:

- Recognize what makes a volcano erupt. See their hearts and not just what they do, but why they do it. I know it's not easy to get past the hurt they cause you, but until you do, there's little hope for healing in your relationship.

- Respond rather than react. Stop to understand them rather than blow up or walk away in disgust. Reacting with your anger is like pouring gas on a raging fire.
- Declare a time-out. Often, time will help the volcano regain control of their emotions. It will also help you compose yourself (Proverbs 29:11). Know when to stop what's going on and then redirect your conversation to a better time and place.
- Take them to God in prayer (Matthew 5:43-45).

Living with or working with a volcano is really difficult. Everything in us wants to either fight back or flee from them. God, however, has a radically different way for us to live. No matter what, we are called to function as children of our Father in heaven.

What next?

Do you deal with a volcano on a regular basis? Next time they explode, pray for God's wisdom, and then respond rather than react.

May I pray for you?

Father, give us your strength to love the unlovely. Give us your grace to be kind to people who don't deserve it and patient with those who hurt us. Give us your heart, so that we might see the brokenness of others as you see them. And help us to be slow to anger and rich in love, just like you. Amen.

DAY 7: GETTING ALONG PART 4: SPONGES

"Love never gives up, never loses faith, is always hopeful, and endures through every circumstance" 1 Cor. 13:7 NLT.

When Laura and I were newlyweds, we lived in an apartment. On one side of us resided a neighbor we'll call Mary. Mary soaked up everyone around her like a dry sponge. She wasn't mean or harsh, but she would emotionally grab on to people and suck the marrow out of them. We felt uncomfortable around her and guilty for avoiding her, but we didn't know what else to do.

Do you have someone like this in your life? Probably. So let's begin with the anatomy of a sponge. They are clingy and needy, and smother their potential friends. They make you feel guilty for failing to rescue them from one perceived crisis to the next. They attach themselves to you like gum stuck to the bottom of a shoe.

Here's what I'm learning about surviving and helping a sponge:

- Empathize—don't just sympathize. Sympathy is to *feel sorry for* someone else. Empathy is to *identify* with and to *understand* another's situation, feelings, and motives.

- Confront when necessary. Often, when you see and understand the *why,* you become aware of a character flaw or sin in the life of a sponge. Assuming you've dealt with your own sin first, there is a place for humble and gentle rebuke (Galatians 6:1). Remember, as a general rule, a sponge believes they are a worthless failure. So try hard to speak into their life in such a way that builds rather than destroys. Be sure to affirm their value as you confront and correct.
- Learn to say *no,* and don't feel guilty about it. It's okay and good to establish healthy boundaries. Sometimes we suffer from a Messiah complex and think we've got to fix people. Even the Son of God found it wise to draw boundaries (see Matthew 14), and I want to suggest you follow his example.

It might cost you to do the right thing for a sponge, but that doesn't mean you should ignore your legitimate needs in the process. Love and serve the sponge in your life, and sometimes that means saying *no.*

What next?
If you have a sponge in your life, think about what boundaries you need to draw, and then focus on loving them as Christ would.

May I pray for you?

God, you have called us to love all people, and that includes those whom we deem a challenge. Give us the tools we need to love effectively and to confront when necessary. Thank you for being our example and loving us far beyond what we can imagine. Amen.

DAY 8: GETTING ALONG PART 5: WHAT IF IT'S *ME*?

"When I refused to confess my sin, I was weak and miserable, and I groaned all day long. Finally, I confessed all my sins to you and stopped trying to hide them. I said to myself, 'I will confess my rebellion to the LORD.' And you forgave me! All my guilt is gone" Psalm 32:3,5.

Many years ago, a man came to me after a service in our church. He was in his 50s, married, and had two sons. With tears in his eyes, he told me about his life. He was a recovering alcoholic. He'd been in prison. His sons despised him. His wife was afraid of him. He had a terrible temper, was as negative and critical as anyone you've ever met, and he was the ultimate control freak.

That day he asked, "Can God change me?" And without hesitation I answered, "Yes, restoration is his specialty!" What's true for him is true for you as well.

Whatever character issues or problems you have right now can be healed and resolved by the transforming power of God in your life. You can change, and there is hope because nothing is too big for the Lord.

Let's take a look at our part in the process:

- Be honest. It's imperative that you take off whatever mask you live behind. The first step toward genuine and lasting change begins with honesty. As long as you live in denial or feign a persona, you hinder the transforming power of God. No one is perfect, so why pretend?
- Get help. It is important to admit that you're broken, but it's not enough. Once you've owned your sin, you need to get the support and encouragement that comes from accountability. You can't do it on your own. This is hard for some of us (most of us) to admit. We are stubbornly autonomous, and we believe that strong people are self-sufficient and weak people require help. What a bunch of hooey! We all need help and it's okay. You are not alone, and you were designed to function best when you are properly related vertically with God and horizontally with others.
- Be patient. The Lord often reminds me: you didn't create this situation or mess overnight, and it might take more than a night to change it and you. You also must be patient with your friends, family, and those who might have written you off as a lost cause. If they've been wounded or abused by you, then the healing of your relationship will take time. Endure.

What next?

God can and will change you and heal your broken relationships, but he needs you to yield to him, to cooperate with him, and to trust the work of his love and power in your life. If you need to be restored, get on your knees and cry out to the Lord today.

May I pray for you?

God, sometimes we fail miserably and repeatedly. Don't let us remain in our sinful state. Change us. Restore us. Heal our broken relationships. We confess our sin and ask for your help. Amen.

DAY 9: IF YOUR CHILD WANDERS

"Meanwhile, the moment we get tired in the waiting, God's Spirit is right alongside helping us along. If we don't know how or what to pray, it doesn't matter. He does our praying in and for us, making prayer out of our wordless sighs, our aching groans" Romans 8:26 TM.

As a son, I know firsthand about wandering from faith. In my early 20s, I rejected everything I once believed. I was the prodigal son who needed and received grace.

As a father, I desire to see my children passionate about their faith. A thousand times I've prayed, "God, light a fire of love for you deep in their hearts that will prevail."

As a pastor, I've talked to hundreds of parents who worry for their wandering children. They feel fear, anger, sorrow, and often shame. "Where did I go wrong? What should I do now?"

Let me suggest seven things to do when your child struggles with his or her faith:

- Bless them! Look for opportunities to demonstrate your love for who they are regardless of what they do. You might be tempted to react in anger, but it's not about you. Find a way to say, "No matter what, I will always love you!"

- Encourage them to ask and wrestle with honest questions about God, and resist the tendency to give them *your* answers. They might be surprised that you are challenging them to argue with God rather than to argue with you!
- Never doubt God's ability to redeem, restore, and renew. Nothing is too hard for God, and no one is too far gone for him to reach.
- Work hard to build relational bridges with your child. You don't have to agree with or like what they do, but don't let your disappointment create a barrier.
- Pray. Pray hard. Pray with thanksgiving too. An important key to developing and maintaining faith and a good attitude starts here. Thank God for your child.
- Watch with hope. Keep your eyes on the horizon looking for their return. Hope, in the biblical sense, is living with a God-confidence no matter what.
- When they do return (and someday they will), accept them in love and with celebration! When they're ready, they will unpack their story with you.

My heart is broken for you if you have a prodigal son or daughter. But don't give up! I'm so grateful that my family and my God never gave up on me.

What next?
If your child has wandered, reach out to them today and start building a bridge back.

May I pray for you?

God, we lift our children to you and ask that you would light a fire in their hearts to follow you whole-heartedly. They are yours. Thank you for taking care of them. Amen.

DAY 10: KEEP IT SIMPLE

"Don't worry about tomorrow. It will take care of itself. You have enough to worry about today" Matthew 6:34 CEV.

I attended a picnic recently and noticed how uncomplicated and free the kids were. They didn't worry about the meat on the BBQ or who brought what for a side dish. They made fun their only concern. It was a picnic after all.

I know as adults we have responsibilities. I understand the need to plan and prepare. But does life have to be so complicated? Let me give you six steps to keep it simple:

- Remember what is and isn't eternal. Only people live forever! That task or thing you're stressing over may not have much (or any) eternal significance. The first step to a simpler life is remembering to focus on what matters most—people.
- Identify and stay true to your core values. What six or seven things best define who you are, your ideals, and your purpose? For example, loving God and others is one of my core values. If an opportunity isn't related to love at some level, I'm not interested. But if I can advance the cause of love, I'm in! Loyalty, faithfulness, and family are other core values to me.
- Try to make a subtraction for every addition in your life. Have you noticed how easy it is to say *yes* and

how hard it is to say *no*? One of the most effective ways to simplify your life is to stop something old whenever you start something new. This step is much easier when you've applied the previous two steps.

- Practice sacrificial generosity. The more we have, the more we worry, and the more we worry, the more complicated our lives become. I'm not saying it's bad to own stuff, but it's a problem when our stuff starts to own us. The best way to guard our hearts against distracting materialism is to give generously.
- Determine which voices you're going to listen to. Sometimes the multitude of other voices are nothing more than diversions. Be humble. Be a good listener. But be wise too, and listen to the voices that matter most.
- Live fully in the moment. It's good to plan for the future. But sometimes we are so future-minded we are of no present good. We can't spend all our time worrying about tomorrow. The simple thing is the present thing. Do it well. Do it now.

What next?
What have you found effective for de-cluttering your life? Pick one or two of the actions above and start simplifying today.

May I pray for you?

God, our society values busyness. We feel worthwhile when we're needed, and oftentimes add more to our plates than we can manage. Refocus our attention on the eternal. Help us simplify our lives. Amen.

DAY 11: THE OLDER I GET

"Even to your old age and gray hairs I am he, I am he who will sustain you. I have made you and I will carry you; I will sustain you and I will rescue you" Isaiah 46:4.

Unless I live to be 115, I have a lot fewer birthdays ahead of me than I do behind me. The funny thing is I don't think of myself as an old guy, and I'm often surprised by the age of the face looking back at me in the mirror. But the marks of maturity are there and undeniable.

My hair is thinning, my belly bulges, my back frequently aches, and my brain sometimes takes a nap while the rest of me remains wide awake. (I think they call them "senior moments," but I can't remember.)

Truth is, I'm comfortable in my skin. I have no desire or plans to color my hair, lipo-suck my belly, or tighten the wrinkles on my face. It is what it is, and I am who I am.

Unless I become the bionic man and get new knees, I'll never run another marathon. Unless they come up with a fat pill that truly does work (I've tried the ones that don't), I will probably always struggle with my weight simply due to a slowing metabolism. And unless I get a brain transplant, someday I might forget more than I remember.

Granted, aging has its downsides, but here are the things

I choose to focus on:

- After 50+ years of doing life, I think I can pass some valuable lessons along to the next generation.
- I see each day as a gift from God, and I waste a lot less time doing meaningless things than I used to.
- The growing pool of people who call me pastor, friend, and even grandpa mean far more to me than any *thing* I have.
- I'm embracing this next season of my life and ministry as an opportunity to do even more of the things I love—mentoring, writing and traveling.
- Whatever weeks, months, or years we have left together, I want to continue to grow more madly in love with my wife and best friend.

Take it from an old guy, life is short, and before you know it, you too will see an old face in the mirror. But it's okay…it's even good. Rather than fight the inevitable, embrace each season of life with gusto! All you really have is *now*, so make the most of this moment and live your life on purpose and with intentionality.

What next?

What are your thoughts on aging? Do you embrace or fight each season of life? Make a list (like the one above) of the benefits to growing older.

May I pray for you?

God, aging is inevitable and part of your plan for us. Help us seek you in every stage of life and to grow in maturity and love as we do. We want to serve you until our dying day! Amen.

DAY 12: THE RAGING BATTLE

"Stay alert! Watch out for your great enemy, the devil. He prowls around like a roaring lion, looking for someone to devour" 1 Peter 5:8 NLT.

Spiritual warfare. Two words you won't find used anywhere in the Bible (but referred to often). Two words that inspire some and terrify others.

So what is spiritual warfare? The Bible describes spiritual warfare as an assault by demonic forces determined to defeat, discourage, and devour us. It can come in the form of temptation or trials. Generally, this demonic attack has very little to do with our choices; it's more about what's done against us by evil forces. When your spiritual, emotional, or physical life is threatened, it may be the enemy, and you might be under attack.

Recognizing you are in a battle will help you overcome it. But besides awareness and being "alert," what else can you do?

- Live in faith rather than fear. The apostle John wrote, "The one who is in you is greater than the one who is in the world" (1 John 4:4). Fear must be replaced by a confidence in God's perfect love, leading to faith in his plan and care.
- Yield to God as you resist the darkness. James, the

brother of Jesus, wrote, "Submit to God. Resist the devil, and he will flee from you" (James 4:7). The first critical step is to submit control of your life to God. When you are walking in his light and in his power, the enemy doesn't just casually saunter away; he runs. Furthermore, the best way to overcome temptation is not to focus on the darkness or the temptation but to walk in the light. Confess your struggle. Get help. Cry out to God for wisdom and strength.

- Pray and fast. Nothing terrifies the enemy more than saints on their knees. The Word is powerful and an effective tool in prayer. And when it comes to fasting, it is my conviction that the purpose is not for you to get God's attention, but for God to get yours.

What next?

Here's the challenge: for the next week, commit to a "Daniel fast" (found in Daniel chapter 10). Essentially, participants give up desserts, meat, and all beverages besides water. Use the time to pray and focus on the Lord.

May I pray for you?

God, it's so easy to forget that we're in the midst of an unseen war. We see the carnage all around us, though. Protect us as we wage battle, with the full assurance that you are the victor. Amen.

DAY 13: WHAT'S YOUR TREASURE?

"We have different gifts, according to the grace given to each of us…" Romans 12:6.

Northern California resident, Steve Tran, bought a lottery ticket while on business in San Jose and then promptly forgot about it. Several days later he woke up at 3:00 a.m. and remembered his purchase. Curious to know the result, he went searching for the lost ticket. Turns out, it was a winner worth a measly $324 million!

And he'd left it in a drawer.

This got me thinking…. How many of us have been given a natural or supernatural treasure from God and it's sitting unused somewhere in a drawer of sorts?

- Once upon a time, people used to comment on your musical gift…but it lies dormant now.
- Once upon a time, your friends told you, "You ought to be a counselor or a pastor someday; you're really good with people." But now you isolate yourself from people who are hurting.
- Once upon a time, kids were drawn to you like moths to a porch light, but you are too preoccupied now to bless the little ones.

- Once upon a time, you used to build creative and beautiful things, but you've stopped expressing yourself with your hands and artistic skill.

God has given each one of us talents and skills. They are special gifts for the benefit of others. They also fill our hearts with joy and a sense of purpose as we give them away. The Apostle Paul wrote in 1 Corinthians 12:7, "To each one the manifestation of the Spirit is given for the common good."

Are you doing what God made you to do? And, if not, what's holding you back? Fear? Laziness? False belief? Your comfort zone? A lack of diligence, determination, or development? Perhaps you are only one decision away from a radical and glorious new you.

What next?

If you're uncertain about what gifts you have, commit to a process of intentional discovery. If you know them, but they've been lying dormant, remember the treasure God's put in your life. Take whatever risks are necessary to rekindle this gift, and give it away for the benefit of others in his kingdom!

May I pray for you?

Lord, you have gifted each one of us with amazing abilities. Don't let them go unused. Help us discover our gifts and then use them for your glory! Amen.

DAY 14: 7 SOLUTIONS FOR CONFLICT

"Love covers a multitude of sins" 1 Peter 4:8.

Occasionally, I get "you suck" emails from people. Sometimes they live far away and their email is in lieu of wasting a postage stamp. But more often than not they live nearby and, for whatever reason, want to avoid personal confrontation.

Whether you've been hurt by a nasty email or are engaged in direct conflict, how should you deal with your frustration and anger? Glad you asked!

- First, bite your lip and count to a million! Try not to react. In fact, under-react. The first thing that comes to mind is rarely the best thing to say when resolving a disagreement. Give it some time before you respond.
- Remember, don't be right at the cost of losing rapport. There's nothing wrong with being right, but you can be right *and* dead wrong if you sacrifice relationship on the altar of pride.
- Zoom out and try to see the bigger picture. Ask yourself this simple, yet powerful, question: *What is really going on here?* Maybe there's an issue behind the issue. Loving others means putting their needs before your own.
- Before you blast them, ask them. In other words,

before you give them an earful, ask them the *why*, *how* and *what* questions. This is the path of humility.

- Listen more than you speak. If possible, set up a time to sit down face-to-face with the goal of listening first and foremost. Often, 90% of the problem is resolved when someone genuinely feels cared for and heard.
- Affirm your love before, during, and after any corrective word is spoken. The most important thing that must result from any relational conflict is a commitment to love each other no matter what.
- If a wall is built to keep you *out*, build a bigger wall to bring them *in*. The difference between your wall and their wall is yours is built to be inclusive and to protect the relationship, not eliminate it.

Unfortunately, I've acquired most of these strategies through multiple and painful relational conflicts. The good news is you don't have to learn everything the hard way.

What next?
Decide now to put these seven relational practices into play next time you're in the middle of an emotional explosion. What have you got to lose?

May I pray for you?
God, nobody knows better than you the pain of rejection and conflict, yet you always respond with love. You died to save us all. Help us love like you do. Amen.

DAY 15: BUMPER CARS

"But he gives us more grace. That is why Scripture says: 'God opposes the proud but shows favor to the humble.' Humble yourselves before the Lord, and he will lift you up" James 4:6,10.

My dear wife was *not* happy with me! Our three grandchildren wanted to ride the bumper cars, and fulfilling their desire required her begrudging participation. I did my best to avoid her car. One bumper-whack from me would have really put me in the doghouse. I smiled at her. She glared at me.

I get motion sickness easily and felt a little woozy after the ride ended. As I attempted to get out of the car, while helping my four-year-old riding partner out as well, I caught my foot on something and ended up sprawled on the floor. I felt embarrassed, very old and foolish. (Not to mention in pain!)

I desperately wanted to blame somebody. Anybody. I wish I could have blamed my wife. But I didn't.

Here's what I'm learning about failure:

- Own it. Just take responsibility. Admit your humanness and your tendency to go left when you should go right. It's okay. Nobody's perfect.

- Confess it. Don't be afraid to say, "I blew it. Please forgive me."
- Don't just *go* through it, *grow* through it. Here's a radical concept: learn from your mistakes!
- Forgive yourself. Forgive others. Don't swallow the poison of bitterness.
- After doing all the above, move on. You don't have to get stuck. Life's too short to live it looking in the rearview mirror.

To my wife's credit, she didn't say, "I told you so." She didn't enjoy the ride, but she also didn't enjoy seeing me get hurt or embarrassed either.

My wife is a lot like Jesus. He won't throw your past blunders in your face. He finds no joy in seeing you suffer. His only hope is that you will grow and learn from your mistakes.

What next?
Think of a recent failure (whether intentional or accidental) and work through the above steps to resolve it.

May I pray for you?
God, give us the grace we need to humble ourselves before you. Don't allow us to wallow in our mistakes; help us grow from them so we will become more like Jesus. Amen.

DAY 16: CHANGING COURSE

"Don't be anxious about anything; rather, bring up all of your requests to God in your prayers and petitions, along with giving thanks. Then the peace of God that exceeds all understanding will keep your hearts and minds safe in Christ Jesus" Philippians 4:6-7 CEB.

Have you ever had those moments when you wanted to go one way only to discover that circumstances beyond your control took you the opposite direction? Have you ever organized an event and nothing went according to your master plan?

Of course you have. We all have. Life happens. Rather than get freaked out when things go sideways, here are some lessons I'm learning about dealing with the unexpected:

- Chill. Take a deep breath and remember, "This too shall pass." Trust me, I realize how hard it is to do this when you're in the midst of a storm. But let me ask you, when has your anxiety ever made a bad situation better? Here's a crazy idea: maybe Jesus was right when he said in Matthew 6:27 (NLT), "Can all your worries add a single moment to your life?" Answer: no. So stop, breathe, and wait patiently on God.
- Step back and look up. I often speak and write about perspective. Why? Because our perspective changes

everything. Typically, when we get lost in the maze of life, it's because we are no longer God-centered or walking in trust. God challenged Jeremiah with these words, "I am the Lord, the God of all mankind. Is anything too hard for me?" (Jer. 32:27 NIV). Answer: no, there is nothing too big for God. So trust in him. Nothing is beyond God's power to redeem, restore, and renew. Nothing.

- Pray your guts out, and pray with praise. Prayer is a huge part of changing your perspective because it turns your attention to God. He can handle your frustration. He knows and understands you better than anyone. And somehow in the weeping and wailing before him, your heart opens to receive his peace.

I know how hard it is to find yourself in a place far from what you ever imagined. But stay fixed on Jesus and hold on. Even when you end up somewhere you never would have chosen—you are not alone—he is with you always.

What next?
Are you facing an unexpected situation? Ask the Lord for his perspective and help.

May I pray for you?
God, as we journey along life's path, the twists and turns in the road often surprise us. Help us trust you to guide us even when we're unsure where the way leads. Amen.

DAY 17: FACING THE UNEXPECTED PART 1

"Look at the proud! They trust in themselves, and their lives are crooked. But the righteous will live by their faithfulness to God" Habakkuk 2:4 NLT.

I never expected to become a pastor. I never expected the devastating loss of my grandson, Phineas. I was shocked when my doctor diagnosed me with prostate cancer in the spring of 2011. Believe me, I could go on and on. Life is chock-full of bewildering and unexpected events.

So what should you do when life throws you a curve? How can we guard our hearts and become better instead of bitter regardless of the struggles in this life?

- Stay tender. Difficulty has a way of leading us into cold-heartedness if we let it. When something we didn't see coming smacks us, we may well become mean and emotionally ugly. Staying tender is not easy when struggles pummel you. That being said, here's the attitude we are challenged to adopt in the Scriptures: "Be kind to each other, tenderhearted, forgiving one another, just as God through Christ has forgiven you" (Ephesians 4:32 NLT).
- Stay faithful. To stay faithful is to stay true, reliable, committed and loyal. In Matthew 25:21 Jesus said, "Well done, good and faithful servant! You have been

faithful with a few things; I will put you in charge of many things...." When the unexpected comes, will we choose to stay the course or be driven off?

- Stay aware. We are in a battle! Sometimes the unexpected happens because we live in a broken world filled with broken people. Sometimes the unexpected happens because we make a boneheaded mistake. I have learned to ask God these three important questions: *Lord, is this the result of something I've done?* If so, I need to repent. *Is it something done to me by someone else?* If so, I need to forgive. *Or is it the enemy?* And if so, I need to resist!

- Stay ready. God has a plan, the question is: are we ready for what he wants to do in us and through us? Genesis 12 introduces us to a man named Abram (later changed to Abraham). God commanded Abe to leave all he knew to go to some yet unrevealed land. Without question, it was an unexpected revelation for Abram, but I believe one of the reasons he is considered the father of faith is because Abe obeyed.

When the unexpected happens, we can react in fear or respond in faith! The choice is ours.

What next?

Expect the unexpected and stay ready. Decide before the struggle what you will do in the struggle, because life doesn't always go the way we want or expect.

May I pray for you?

God, we can't always see what's ahead. When life smacks us in the face, help us run to you first. May we stay tender, faithful, aware, and ready for whatever plans you have in store. Amen.

DAY 18: FACING THE UNEXPECTED PART 2

"And let us run with perseverance the race marked out for us, fixing our eyes on Jesus, the pioneer and perfecter of faith. For the joy set before him he endured the cross, scorning its shame, and sat down at the right hand of the throne of God" Hebrews 12:2.

Have you ever noticed how just about every television drama wraps things up in the last ten minutes of the show? For the first fifty minutes or so, the trauma is created, the characters are defined, and then just after the last commercial break, the solution is revealed, and the world is well again.

Wouldn't it be nice if that happened in real life? In my experience, life is messy, answers are often elusive, and tidy bows seldom get wrapped around my problems. More often than not, the resolution of our struggle takes days, weeks, months, or even decades.

Of course, I have faith in God. Certainly, I do my best to keep my eyes fixed on him. And yes, I pray. But sometimes it's hard to stay the course. Especially when the journey takes far longer than I want or expect. So what can we do when life doesn't go as expected?

- Decide *now* what you will do *then*. Waiting until

you're at the end of your rope to determine to trust God is probably not a good idea. I've found it best to enter into a hardship with this attitude: no matter what it takes or how long the battle, I will lean on the one who has promised to never leave or forsake me.

- Immerse yourself in truth and hold on. One of the sad realities about "the valley of the shadow of death" is how easy it is to fall into false beliefs when we're in the dark. Find the truth and stand on it regardless of how you feel.

- Surround yourself with people who will hold you up and hold you accountable. Alone, we lose our way. Alone, we get deceived. Alone, we cannot survive. Together, however, we will find the strength to carry on.

- Obtain and maintain an attitude of gratitude. This is perhaps our greatest challenge when the storm rages. I know from experience how hard this is to do. Finding something (anything) to be grateful for is tough. However, one of the greatest assets we can acquire is a thankful heart. We don't have to be thankful *for* everything, but the Word challenges us to be thankful *in* everything (1 Thess. 5:18).

What next?

Take a moment and decide how you will face your next crisis. Write down your thoughts and keep them as a reminder.

May I pray for you?

God, our lives are not 60-minute television shows that wrap up in tidy endings. Sometimes we suffer, struggle, and wait what feels like ages for even small solutions to our problems. Help us trust you regardless and to finish our race strong. Amen.

DAY 19: LIVING THE ADVENTURE!

"For the eyes of the Lord range throughout the earth to strengthen those whose hearts are fully committed to him" 2 Chronicles 16:9.

When a force of energy encounters an immobilized object, something must give. When God encounters us (he being the ultimate force), we either embrace what he has for us or we resist it.

- I'd rather be moving than stuck in the mud.
- I'd rather be energized by God's Spirit than be a cold stone of opposition.
- I'd rather experience the new and even the unknown rather than the "safety" of the old, the stale, the familiar, and the comfortable.

God is creative. He is fresh. Like his mercies, his plan for us is new every morning. But to experience his life and his destiny starts with one word: *yes*!

Yes, have your way in me, Father. Yes, lead me by your Spirit. Yes, show me your path, and I will pursue you with all my heart today! This is the adventure we are meant for, and this is life in the Spirit.

To have God's vision for your life is to imagine something new, better, and different. Sometimes it is to see what others might not see or to hear what others might not hear.

To have a dream is to be driven by a passion to use your God-given gifts to make a difference. Vision is what gets us up in the morning, and it keeps us going in the valley of the shadow of death! Without one, we perish, but with one, we flourish. And for the record, a godly vision will always humble you, and it might even break your heart.

Big or small, do you have a vision for today? Are you following God's dream for your life? Are you willing to let go of the known and venture into the unknown with his Spirit empowering you to do the HIMpossible? Are you willing to say *yes* and if not, why not?

What's holding you back? Worry? Fear? Please remember this: the burden of worry comes from the beast of fear, but love destroys the beast. Live in his perfect love today.

What next?
Today, pray that God would renew his vision for you. Then say *yes!*

May I pray for you?
God, sometimes we are afraid of following you. We're unsure where your path may take us, and we worry about the unknowns along the way. Change our hearts and attitudes from fear to obedience and trust. Remind us of the adventure that awaits! Amen.

DAY 20: MARRIAGE MACE

"Do nothing out of selfish ambition or vain conceit. Rather, in humility value others above yourselves" Philippians 2:3.

I have the privilege of mentoring a group of men who are all young enough to be my sons. Recently, I shared with them about four challenges guaranteed to mess up a marriage. Come to think of it, each of these nasty things will mess up all of your relationships, married or not.

The four things I want to cover here can easily be remembered by recalling the word *mace*. Whether you think of the chemical spray or the ancient weapon, remember that mace destroys.

- M = Me-Centeredness. Most of us have a bad habit of taking care of numero uno first and foremost. In a marriage, selfishness is a leviathan that will destroy our trust and create a lot of tension.
- A = Arrogance. It's bad enough that we have a hard time dying to self, but the fact that we don't really *want* to typically indicates pride. King Solomon wrote, "Pride goes before destruction" (Proverbs 16:18). And in our relationships, arrogance is horribly destructive.
- C = Comparison. If you want to ruin a moment, compare your spouse to your coworker or your

best friend's spouse and get ready for an explosion of frustration. Depending on your partner's nature, that frustration may play itself out as depression or anger, but whatever the emotion, it won't be pretty. Comparison devalues who we are and takes us out of the realm of unconditional love into a performance-based relationship.

- E = Egregious Expectations. Egregious expectations are wants, desires, and needs that aren't reasonable. Of course, we all have expectations. But when those expectations are unreasonable and unmet we have a huge problem. Even if the expectation *is* reasonable and rational, how we handle disappointment matters too. The challenge we face in our relationships is to manage our unmet expectations with grace and to honestly evaluate all our expectations with wisdom.

Like I said, we will face plenty of other challenges in our relationships, but none more harmful than *MACE*. So ask God for his help and strength to be the man or woman you need and want to be.

What next?
Today, put your spouse above yourself and tell him/her how much you appreciate them.

May I pray for you?
God, when we focus on you, our relationships benefit. Be first in our lives. Amen.

DAY 21: PLASTIC JESUS

"Though he was God, he did not think of equality with God as something to cling to. Instead, he gave up his divine privileges; he took the humble position of a slave and was born as a human being" Philippians 2:6-7 NLT.

Every Christmas, we pull out our collection of nativity scenes. Some of them have been passed down to us from our family, others have been received as gifts, and we bought a nice one in an after-Christmas sale a few years ago.

My favorite nativity, however, is a plastic one made by Mattel. It's a toy made for children, and all the little characters are indestructible. It has a cool angel who sits on top of the barn, and when you bop her on the head, the song *Away in a Manger* plays. Unfortunately, we lost the Joseph piece years ago, and Mary is now a single mom (which makes her even more valuable to me).

Of course, Jesus is a plastic baby, lying in a plastic manger, surrounded by a plastic barn, being adored by a plastic shepherd and plastic animals. But the whole thing is just so stinkin' cute I want to play with it as much as my grandchildren do.

One morning as I sat in my favorite chair for a little time alone with the Lord, I looked up from my Bible to see plastic Jesus on my coffee table (precariously close to the edge). It struck me: Jesus didn't come to a castle or mansion; he gave up everything for you and me. He left the true riches and vast glory of heaven to become a child born to a poor blue-collar family. And he did this so we could know him, relate to him, and fall in love with him.

Without a doubt, if Jesus went shopping today to buy a nativity scene to celebrate his birthday, it wouldn't be one made out of gold or silver…it'd be plastic. Something simple, humble, raw and real, just like him.

What next?
Today, be content. Look for ways to serve. Focus on the eternal, not on the temporal.

May I pray for you?
Jesus, you are the son of the most-high God. As such, you could have come to earth as a conquering king, a privileged prince, an omnipotent ruler. Instead, you came as a baby. A humble servant of all. May we follow your example. Amen.

DAY 22: REGRETS

"Brothers and sisters, I don't consider that I have taken hold of it yet. But here is the one thing I do. I forget what is behind me. I push hard toward what is ahead of me. I move on toward the goal to win the prize. God has appointed me to win it. The heavenly prize is Christ Jesus himself" Philippians 3:13-14 NIRV.

We humans spend a lot of time looking back. And I don't mean just taking a peek once in a while in the rear-view mirror; I mean a full-bodied-turn-around to what was. We sometimes long for the good-ol'-days. We often wish things could be the way they were, or tragically, we look back in regret and wish those times never happened.

Of course, we know we can't undo the past, but we still spend a lot of time wishing we could. Our hearts and minds are consumed by a dump truck full of "if onlys."

- If only I was younger….
- If only I didn't marry that person….
- If only I had stayed in school….
- If only I had said *yes*, or maybe *no*….
- If only I had a chance to do it all over again….

What if instead of looking back we learned to live fully alive in the present? What if we learned from our past and then applied those lessons in the here and now without guilt? What if we experienced the presence and power of God in this very moment?

Certainly, my past influences my present and future, but it does not control it. I do. I can choose right now to surrender all the good, the bad, the beautiful, and even the ugly of my history to God. I can choose to trust in his ability to use whatever has happened in my life for his purposes today. I can choose to believe that when I live in him, for him, and by him, the boundaries of my past do not have to become the horizons of my present or my future.

To live lost in the past is crazy. To live fully alive in the present is wise. To have hope for my future in Christ is awesome. So live in the moment.

What next?
Today, choose to live in the now. Live in Jesus knowing the freedom and joy of his presence in your present.

May I pray for you?
God, our lives on earth are "but a breath." We want to leverage every moment you give us instead of wasting time dwelling on regrets. Show us how to live in the present. Give us the wisdom and fortitude to seize each day as we walk with you. Amen.

DAY 23: SELAH

"There's an opportune time to do things, a right time for everything on the earth: ...a right time to hold on and another to let go..." Ecclesiastes 3:1, 6 TM.

Life is crazy. Now more than ever, we possess the ability to do more things with more gadgets supposedly designed to make our lives easier. And yet, this increase in opportunity comes with a decrease in margin.

Margin is defined as the space between. It's the blank space on the page of a book. It's the surplus pavement on the road between the white and yellow lines. It's the extra ten minutes we add to our commute in case of bad traffic.

Without margin, too many words on a page overwhelm us. Without margin, we get nervous about hitting another car or driving into the ditch. Without margin, we tend toward chronic tardiness. Without margin, life can make us insane.

One of my favorite words in the book of Psalms is *Selah*. Selah is a margin term. In fact, most believe it is a musical expression instructing the singer to take an interlude or a break. Why? To give you time to reflect, pause, and breathe.

Selah is margin. It allows us to stop and think, to ponder

and wonder. It gives us a moment to consider what has happened, is happening and might happen in our lives. It allows us to turn our hearts toward something better.

By the way, margins don't miraculously materialize; you have to make them. You and you alone can hit the pause button in your life.

You might be a mom with three kids and a schedule that competes with any CEO. You might be a student working part-time, going to school full-time, and trying to enjoy a social life in the midst of it all. You might really be a CEO! Regardless of your role or the number of plates you're spinning, you must carve out margin to survive.

Margin gives us strength and perspective, and that's why you need space and a regular Selah.

What next?
Intentionally put a power nap into your afternoon. Decide to take a walk before you jump into the pile on your desk. Choose to block out time each and every day to simply sit and stare out the window and reflect on life. It's okay. It really is.

May I pray for you?
God, with all our high-tech gadgets at hand, most of us are constantly connected to the ethos. Help us create margin in our lives so that we can better serve you! Amen.

DAY 24: THE TRIBE

"So now you Gentiles are no longer strangers and foreigners. You are citizens along with all of God's holy people. You are members of God's family" Ephesians 2:19 NLT.

I'm a paleface. As far as I know, no Native American blood runs through my veins. The closest I've ever come to smoking a peace pipe was taking a hit off my dad's tobacco pipe (not a good idea when you're ten, by the way). I never wanted to be a cowboy when we played cowboys and Indians as a kid. Indians are cool; cowboys drool.

I saw something not long ago that got me thinking about how the Church should be more like a tribe than a temple. The Church is not a building, a business venture, or a 501c3 non-profit organization—it's supposed to be a community of faith—a tribe if you will. In fact, there are some very strong similarities to church and a Native American tribe:

- Tribes share a common identity. In fact, they take great pride in their tribal history, customs and language. As a tribe, the Church holds a common history, customs and even a language of sorts. Our past may not always look pretty, but warts and all, the blood of Jesus connects us.

- Tribes stick together. The identity of a tribe unites them. When the tribe flourishes, everyone flourishes. When the tribe suffers, everyone suffers. When the tribe moves, everyone moves. The tribe functions together in a partnership where each section does its part for the sake of the whole.
- Tribes honor their elders. From the time they are infants, each member of the tribe is taught the value of honoring the tribal elders. The young and restless are challenged to heed the advice of the old and experienced. Unfortunately, in our society we devalue age and elevate youth. So the young don't tend to listen, and the old work hard to hide their gray. Maybe it's time for us to embrace the words of Solomon, one of the wisest guys to ever live, who said, "The glory of the young is their strength; the gray hair of experience is the splendor of the old," (Proverbs 20:29 NLT).

What next?

How have you connected with your tribe lately? Be intentional this week about engaging in the Church.

May I pray for you?

Jesus, you intended for your Bride to exist as many parts and yet one body. We belong to the same family, the same tribe, regardless of which branch we adhere to. Help us maximize our community and minimize our differences for your glory. Amen.

DAY 25: ALL MY FATHERS

"God, you see trouble and sadness. You take note of it. You do something about it.... You help children whose fathers have died" Psalm 10:14 NIRV.

My dad, George Bubna, had plenty of issues. For most of my life we weren't very close, and conflict filled our relationship. During his last few years, however, he changed and I finally felt proud to call him Dad.

Al Battles, my father-in-law, was a small and gentle man. I think having raised four daughters and no sons made Al wonder at times what to do with me. In many ways, we were polar opposites. But he knew I loved his daughter, and I knew he loved me.

Frank Mayo became my stepdad in my late twenties. At first, I felt uneasy about gaining a stepfather. He was about as different from my natural father as he could get. But for over a quarter of a century, Frank loved me as his son.

All three of my dads have passed, and I deeply miss them. But during the times I feel most lonely, I hear the Holy Spirit whisper to my heart, "Kurt, you *have* never and you *will* never be without a Father."

God sees. He knows. He understands. And he is a father to the fatherless. He comforts and helps children, even old children like me, whose fathers have died.

How do you feel about your relationship with your dad(s)? If you're a father, are you pleased with the connection you maintain with your kids?

I thank God for the influence each of my dads had in my life. I long for the day when I will be with them again. Until then, and beyond then, I am not alone. Never. Abba Father is always close to me.

What next?
Today, call the father figures in your life and let them know how much you love and appreciate them. If you need to mend a broken relationship, ask the Lord to help you. And if you're without a dad, lean into the one who is Father of all.

May I pray for you?
God, comfort those of us whose earthly fathers are no longer present in our lives. Help us heal from the pain of loss and allow you to fill the void in our hearts. Thank you for being our ever-present Dad. Amen.

DAY 26: OVERCOMING FEAR

"God is our refuge and strength, an ever-present help in trouble. Therefore we will not fear, though the earth give way and the mountains fall into the heart of the sea, though its waters roar and foam and the mountains quake with their surging" Psalm 46:1-3.

Banks Fold! Market Crashes! Millions Lose All!

What if the headlines above were true? What if the relative affluence of the western world became a distant and haunting memory?

When you live in a country with over 18 trillion dollars of debt (as of 2014), it's not hard to imagine the shoe dropping soon and hard. Our American economy is a paper tiger, and it doesn't take much for a paper tiger to go up in flames.

If you're like me, you find this a frightening reality. And fear is a powerful de-motivator.

- If you're afraid of getting eaten by a shark, you might not spend much time in the ocean.
- If you're afraid of heights, you probably won't go parachuting anytime soon.
- If you're afraid of ending up in the poor house, you may not give sacrificially.

Fear causes us to hoard rather than help. Fear causes us to stay rather than go. Fear cripples. So what's the answer?

First, maybe it's time to reprioritize what truly matters. The Bible makes it clear our focus belongs on God and his kingdom. Jesus said, "Seek first the kingdom of God and his righteousness…" (Matthew 6:33). When we put the kingdom of God first, we live with faith; when we don't, we live in fear.

The second answer to the beast of fear is to remember: *God is with us.* Always. He is our refuge, our strength, and our help even when everything around us falls to pieces.

I don't know what the future holds, but this much I do know: God holds our future. So do your best to put him first and live in the shelter of his care.

What next?
What are you afraid of? Today, seek first the kingdom of God. Bring your fear to the Lord, and trust him with it.

May I pray for you?
God, we live in uncertain times. Whether we're experiencing unrest in our relationships, with our finances, or with other uncontrollable, global worries, we often lose sight of you. Help us reprioritize our focus and trust you. Amen.

DAY 27: FORGIVENESS

"Peter came to Jesus and asked, 'Lord, how many times shall I forgive my brother when he sins against me? Up to seven times?' Jesus answered, 'I tell you, not seven times, but seventy-seven times'" Matthew 18:21-22.

She was in my face and spitting fire!

"Are you telling me I have to forgive my ex-husband? You have no idea what he's done to me!"

Actually, I did have a pretty good idea of the tragic and heartbreaking abuse she'd suffered. Nonetheless, I told her what I've learned from firsthand experience: we forgive because we've been forgiven, and we forgive so that *we* can live free.

Learning to forgive (yourself or others) is perhaps the single most important key to long-term health and happiness.

In our gut we know sin requires judgment. That's why we demand punishment for law-breakers. So when God steps into our lives with his mercy, grace and forgiveness, something in us goes on tilt. It's easier to pay penance than to fully accept God's grace.

Here's what the Bible says, "If we confess our sins to him,

God can be depended on to forgive us and to cleanse us from every wrong" (1 John 1:9 TLB).

Too often, we listen to the voice of the "accuser." You don't have to be a Christian very long to realize that our enemy works against our acceptance of God's mercy. We must learn to tune out the accuser and listen only to the voice of our Father who loves us like crazy!

Forgiveness is hard. Learning to walk in a lifestyle of forgiveness isn't for the faint of heart, but it is the secret to your heart's healing.

What next?

Are you currently struggling to forgive yourself or someone else? Are you hesitant to accept forgiveness? Decide today that you will live a lifestyle of forgiveness. If you need help, talk to a trusted friend or pastor.

May I pray for you?

Father, teach us to forgive as we have been forgiven. Help us learn to recognize your voice above our own self-talk, the voices of others, and the voice of the enemy. Cause our lives to be marked by your mercy in such a powerful way that others see you in us and are drawn to your grace. Amen.

DAY 28: HARD KNOCKS

"Here on earth you will have many trials and sorrows. But take heart, because I have overcome the world" John 16:33 NLT.

Life is hard. Of course, life is often good too, but there's no denying the struggle most of us face on a regular basis.

- You don't get the promotion or raise you deserve.
- Your spouse says, "I want a divorce."
- You suffer a miscarriage.
- The doctor says, "I'm afraid this is going to require surgery and a long recovery period."
- An in-law becomes an outlaw.

So what have I learned about life and hardship?

- I've learned to expect the unexpected.
- I've learned to stay the course no matter what the course may bring.
- I've learned that I'm not nearly as godly or Christ-like as I need to be.
- I've learned that grace includes the Lord's incredible patience with me.
- I've learned to be humble and dependent on the Father for everything.
- I've learned to fix my eyes and heart on Christ. He has never left me.

- I've learned that God can handle my questions.

Read this next part very slowly: God never promised us an easy life. He never assured us an answer to everything, not on this side of eternity. If that were the case, how would hope and faith play into the mix? The normal expectation for Christ-followers is faith in the face of the unknown and trust even when we are baffled by life.

Is it easy? No. But here's the last thing I want you to hear: though we have no guarantee of an easy life, we do have the promise of his presence. No matter what, we are never alone and never left to wade through the mud and muck in our own strength. (Check out Hebrews 13:5 and Psalm 23:4.)

What next?
What's the hardest thing you are facing right now? You are not alone even when surrounded by darkness and despair. You can't know everything, but you are always connected to the one who knows all things. So hold on, especially when life is hard.

May I pray for you?
God, thank you for walking with us through our darkest hours. Thank you for being faithful to us. Help us lean into you when we don't understand your plan, and to trust your guidance when we can't see the path ahead. Amen.

DAY 29: HOW TO SUCCEED

"His master replied, 'Well done, good and faithful servant! You have been faithful with a few things; I will put you in charge of many things. Come and share your master's happiness!'" Matthew 25:21.

Several years ago, a discouraged middle-aged man named Tom came to see me. He said, "I've spent my entire life trying to succeed at something...*anything*...but the golden ring is always just out of reach."

I asked him an important question, "Tell me, how do you define success?" Without blinking, he rattled off a list of measurable goals he wanted to accomplish. Most of them related to numbers and recognition by his peers. I gently pushed back and asked, "What if success is different than you think?" The look on his face was telling as I took five minutes to explain how God defines success.

- In God's economy, success is faithful obedience. We often measure prosperity by the size of our assets or the accolades given to us by others. For God, it's all about the choice to follow his path regardless of the financial or public rewards. We make God smile when we take risks and exercise faith in our pursuit of his kingdom.
- In God's kingdom, success involves embracing our weaknesses. Too many believe that success requires

strength. I disagree. I suggest that to be strong we must recognize our frailty and how desperately we need God's help. The path to success does not deny our weakness; instead, it embraces it in humble dependence on the Holy Spirit.

- God measures achievement by our resiliency. I know it sounds cliché, but our success is more about the journey, not the final destination. As Christ-followers, what we learn in and through the struggle of life on planet earth is important. God honors those who run with endurance, finish the race, and keep the faith (Hebrews 12:1-2; 2 Timothy 4:7).

My friend, Tom, had an "aha moment" when he realized he'd been pursuing a culturally-defined idea of accomplishment rather than a God-defined objective for his life.

What next?
What are your core values? Do they line up with God's definition of success?

May I pray for you?
Father, the world often teaches us something counter to your revelation. Help us to unlearn what is contrary to your Word and your ways. Reveal the truth, truth that will set us free to see your kingdom come and your will accomplished on the earth as it is in heaven. Amen.

DAY 30: PET PEEVES

"Love your enemies, do good to them…. Then your reward will be great, and you will be children of the Most High, because he is kind to the ungrateful and wicked" Luke 6:35.

We all have things that push our buttons and tick us off. Even the kindest among us complain at times about practices we deem foolish or frustrating. Most of my pet peeves relate to the stupid or rude driving habits of others, but here's my *biggest* grievance: when we make our pet peeves more important than people.

We get frustrated when the other seven billion people on the planet aren't nearly as smart as we are. Sadly, we justify our anger when the selfish or ignorant trample on our desires.

I've allowed some of the meanest and most ungodly words to escape my mouth while driving. Some time ago I stopped honking my horn in anger, after I did so to a parishioner in my church (that was embarrassing), but if Jesus rode shotgun with me he'd be disappointed with my language.

How would my attitude be different, and my words kinder, if I valued people more than my pet peeves? What would it be like if I put the needs of others before my own?

By no means am I excusing immoral or foolish behavior. Of course, there's right and wrong, and laws should be obeyed for the common good. But when we violently lash out at others when they cross a line, we cross into sin. When we return evil for evil, we become the ones in error.

What's *your* pet peeve? Tattoos? Loud worship music? Pit bulls? Preachers in jeans? Parents who bring kids to R-rated movies? Beer? Homosexuals? People who throw gum on a sidewalk? Jerks who take up two parking spots? Democrats? Republicans? Bad spelllors? ☺

What ticks you off so much that your reaction reveals your love for being *right* more than your love for being *relational*? Without question, Jesus held high standards and was always right, but he loved even the wicked because that's what love does. You can have your pet peeve, but please don't make it more important than acting like Jesus.

What next?
Today, look past irritations, inconveniences and ignorance, and focus on loving others like Jesus does.

May I pray for you?
God, teach us love like you do. When faced with foolishness and wrongdoing, may we choose to respond with the same grace and compassion you have shown us. Amen.

DAY 31: HOLDING ON PART 1

"Even when I walk through the darkest valley, I fear no danger because you are with me" Psalm 23:4.

She looked at me with hopelessness in her eyes as deep as the ocean. Then she screamed through her tears, "What's the point of hoping my husband will change when he's more abusive now than ever before?"

Have you ever held on to a dream for so long that it's become a nightmare? Your dreams, your prayers, and your promises from God seem to mock you and fill you with despair.

Will my son ever be free of drugs? Will I ever get pregnant? Will I ever find a spouse?

If one more person tells you to hold on, you're going to hurt somebody! You're tired of the struggle and exhausted from sleepless nights filled with worry. Nothing in you wants to go through another day of wondering and waiting. You love God, but you're not sure he's paying any attention to your life, so you've withdrawn.

I humbly propose two things for your consideration:

- You are not alone in that valley of darkness (even though you feel like you are).

- You only need to take the next step.

I understand telling someone they are not alone can be irritating when they feel abandoned. There's a part of us that wants to blame God for our predicament, so being told, "He is with you" makes us even madder and more frustrated. But I know I have never truly been alone. Neither are you. Just face the next minute and the next hour…one step at a time.

Hold on or give up? The choice is yours, and you are loved no matter what, but you will never regret pressing on.

What next?

Today, get up and take one step forward. Choose to journey in the right direction even when you feel desperate and afraid. You might take several steps backwards in the process, but press on because the alternative is worse.

May I pray for you?

Father, sometimes in anguish we pray the prayer of Jesus, 'Take this cup from me!" because we're terrified. Sometimes we feel lost and stuck in the swamp of our struggles. Sometimes we wonder if you care or if you're really there in the shadows of our misery. Help us. Hold us. Somehow, by your grace, empower us to take the next step even when we are afraid, empty, and weak. We are desperate for you. Amen.

DAY 32: HOLDING ON PART 2

"Rejoice always, pray continually, give thanks in all circumstances…" 1 Thessalonians 5:16-18.

Years ago I wrestled through the painful loss of a staff member. For over five years he faithfully served as a member of my team. I watched him grow and develop into a gifted pastor. But after he betrayed my trust, we mutually decided upon his resignation. His departure broke my heart.

So how do we hold on through agonizing circumstances?

At the risk of sounding trite or just slapping a "Jesus-sticker" on a very difficult situation, let me tell you what I've learned about holding on even when it's hard.

- We choose where we focus. We can focus on the problem. We can focus on a person. We can choose to get lost in our anger and frustration, or we can choose to seek God. We must decide that no matter what, we will "fix our eyes on Jesus, the pioneer and perfecter of faith (who) for the joy set before him endured the cross" (Hebrews 12:2).
- We guard our hearts. In tough situations it's easy to become embittered and vile. It's okay to be hurt. It's even okay to be angry. But we must "not sin in our anger and not let the sun go down while we're still

angry" (Ephesians 4:26).
- We find something (anything) to be thankful for in the midst of our pain. The power of thankfulness cannot be understated. There is something amazing that happens to our souls when we decide to give thanks to God even when everything in us is screaming out in anguish.

I lost sleep over the exit of that staff member. I wept a river of tears. But I clung to the one who has never let me down, I examined my own heart, and I offered a sacrifice of praise to Jesus in the midst of my angst. And as I did, I found my rest and peace in the Lord.

What next?
Where are you struggling? Where have you been hurt? Where has your heart been broken? May I gently encourage you to press on as you hold on? God will never let you down.

May I pray for you?
Lord, people can and will fail us. (And we can and will fail others!) We may find our circumstances painful, disappointing or unexpected. But as we give you each situation, you are faithful to see us through it. Thank you for being our rock amidst the storms of life. Amen.

DAY 33: PULLING THE "GOD CARD"

"I keep asking that the God of our Lord Jesus Christ, the glorious Father, may give you the Spirit of wisdom and revelation, so that you may know him better" Ephesians 1:17.

You've heard it many times, and so have I, *"The Lord told me...."* And that response is supposed to quiet the critics or explain some bold leap of faith.

Let me be clear: I *do* believe God speaks. I know the value of that "still small voice" of the Spirit. Many times, I have personally heard the Lord in my heart giving me direction. But I also know that people do crazy things in the name of the Lord. I've seen lives, families, and ministries destroyed because something foolish and wrong was executed under a "Thus Saith the Lord" banner.

Here are some guidelines to consider before pulling out the "God card":

- Is it biblical? Trust me, God is never going to contradict himself. He'll never tell you to lie, cheat, steal, or abuse. If it's clear in the Word of God, then that trumps anything you think you've heard.
- Is it wise? God has given us his Word that is full of truth and wisdom. Yes, there are times when what God asks you to do will contradict the wisdom of this

world, but it will not be unwise.

- Is it confirmed by godly elders and pastors in the Body of Christ? Any one of us can find friends to support our outlandish ideas (check out 1 Kings 12). Every good decision I've made in my life and ministry came after counsel from my pastors. They know God, know me, and know wisdom. The Bible expects us to submit to godly authority in our lives.

Listen to God. Expect him to lead and direct you by his Spirit. Trust and believe in him. But never simply pull the "God card" as an excuse to do whatever *you* think you should do. If it is God, it will line up with Scripture, it will be wise, and those in biblical authority who know you best will confirm it.

What next?

When God speaks to you, check the Word, check your heart, check it for wisdom, and check with your pastor before you do anything. This is God's way, and it will protect you from error and foolishness.

May I pray for you?

God, we ask that you give us the Spirit of wisdom and revelation in order to recognize your voice when we hear it. We want to seek you through your Word, Lord, so we may know you fully. Help us walk in your will with confidence. Amen.

DAY 34: A FRIEND IS....

"A friend loves at all times. He is there to help when trouble comes" Proverbs 17:17 NIRV.

Over the years, I've had the fun-tastic pleasure of taking several motorcycle trips with great friends. Nothing puts a smile on my face more than riding the back roads of God's country with the wind in my face and surrounded by buddies.

We laugh. We play. We ride hard. We see beauty beyond description and enjoy the delight of companionship.

Once on the way home from a trip, I thought about what makes a good friend. Here are some ideas I came up with:

- A friend is someone who invests time in the relationship.
- A friend is someone who listens (even when they've heard *that* story 100 times).
- A friend is someone who protects you by pointing out the dangerous gravel and potholes along the way.
- A friend is someone who willingly shares with you (especially when you forget sunscreen or anything to clean your bug-smattered bike).
- A friend is someone who might tease you about snoring, but they'd never really complain.
- A friend is someone who is unafraid to say hard

things in love.
- A friend is someone who looks you in the eye and says, "I love ya, man!" and you know they mean it.

What other qualities of a good friend can you think of? Do you possess these qualities as well? If you lack these traits, it's never too late to develop them. (Start today!)

What next?

If you read this and thought about a good buddy, thank Jesus for that person, and pick up the phone to invite them to coffee soon.

If you read this and wish you had a friend, follow the advice my momma gave me decades ago, "If you want a friend, be friendly, and find someone looking for a friend just like you."

May I pray for you?

Jesus, thank you for modeling perfect friendship so that by imitating you we can become friends who love at all times and help when trouble comes. Continue to show us how to serve each other in ways that please you. Amen.

DAY 35: LIFE IS GOOD?

"In this world you will have trouble. But take heart! I have overcome the world" John 16:33.

Have you ever seen the *Life is Good* line of clothing and hats? Does it make you wonder if life really is that great? Is life good when you lose your job? Is life good when your mom is in the hospital with a serious health problem? Is life good when your unmarried teenage daughter tells you she's pregnant?

We may not say it out loud, but deep in our western Christian culture lies the false belief that God blesses the good and curses the bad. If you're rich, fat and happy, then obviously you're doing something right. If you have a good job, good health, and lots of money in the bank, you must be in the center of God's will. But if you're poor, pathetic and miserable, you probably deserve it. You've almost certainly messed up somewhere along the way and are far from God's intended path.

Part of the problem with this magical-type thinking is how we define blessing. For us, blessing means life is easy, free from stress, and we're flowing in the dough, baby! For some crazy reason, we've bought into a *health and wealth* mentality that expects a smooth path if we're following Jesus. Here's our logic: if it's hard, it can't be God.

Where did we get the ridiculous idea that if it were God's will it would always be easy?

More often than not, what I read in the Scriptures indicates that struggles, trials, and hardships are very common for those who pursue God's agenda and are right in the center of his will.

Let me be clear: I do believe life is good because I believe God is good. Yes, he does want to bless and care for his kids. But we can't afford to define blessing and goodness as living free from difficulty and pain. Maybe, just maybe, God has a bigger plan than you can see, and maybe he's doing a deeper work than you can know.

What next?
Examine the difficulties in your life. Can you see God at work through them, or believe in his goodness even in your badness?

May I pray for you?
Lord, you are good! In our joys and sorrows you are good. In our pain and pleasure you are good. In our poverty and prosperity you are good. You gave us life that we might live it for you, and that's good too! Don't let us forget. Amen.

DAY 36: MONEY MADNESS

"Keep your lives free from the love of money and be content with what you have…" Hebrews 13:5.

I like to shop. (There goes any manly-man reputation I might have had.) For me, shopping is like hunting, so maybe that redeems my rep. I also enjoy people-watching. I get a kick out of husbands being dragged along like they're on a death march, and I even like to window shop. I know…weird.

During a recent trip to California I visited South Coast Plaza. It's off-the-charts stupid cool. It boasts of everything from a lowly Sears to Saks Fifth Avenue, and of course, the classics like Nordstrom and Bloomingdale's. It's three shopping levels of heaven or hell, depending on your perspective.

For most of the morning, I sat at a Starbucks in the mall reading, writing, and simply watching one high roller after another walk by with arms full of Gucci, Prada, and Salvatore Ferragamo.

And you know what I noticed? Not one of them seemed truly happy or content. As the ladies click-clacked by me in their expensive high heels and extremely fashionable clothes, not one of them smiled. Honestly, I can't remember when I've seen so many unhappy people in one place (except for the last time I stood in line at the DMV).

For many in our world, shopping at South Coast Plaza would be a dream come true, but most of the folks I saw looked miserable. It got me thinking, *Maybe Gucci is more like gotcha. Maybe Rolex is for losers, not winners.*

Jesus put it this way, "Whoever wants to be my disciple must deny themselves and take up their cross and follow me. For whoever wants to save their life will lose it, but whoever loses their life for me will find it. What good will it be for someone to gain the whole world, yet forfeit their soul? Or what can anyone give in exchange for their soul?" (Matthew 16:24-26).

I'm not saying that all wealthy people are lost and losers, but Jesus did say, "We can have everything, and yet nothing of any eternal value" (my paraphrase). So if you happen to be rich, be wise, and make sure what you own doesn't own you. And if you're poor, be content; money truly isn't everything.

What next?
Take inventory of your inner wish list. Are you content and thankful for what you have? Do you need to adjust your priorities? Make sure the Lord comes first.

May I pray for you?

God, the world dangles carrots in front of our faces that distract us from what matters. Keep our eyes focused on you and our hearts content with what you give us. We want to pursue you and the eternal, not temporary pleasures. Amen.

DAY 37: TALLY-HO!

"Here's what I want you to do. While I'm locked up here, a prisoner for the Master, I want you to get out there and walk—better yet, run!—on the road God called you to travel. I don't want any of you sitting around on your hands" Ephesians 4:1 TM.

You were made for adventure! Some of you read that and thought, "Whatever. Here he goes again trying to push me out of my nice, safe bubble." You're comfortable. Content. Satisfied. The last thing you want to read about is excitement and uncertainty.

I understand. For many, adventure is synonymous with struggle, hardship, and pain. The word dials up images of someone attempting to climb Mt. Everest or swim the English Channel. We might like to watch the documentaries or read about it in *The Call of the Wild*, but we prefer to experience daring acts vicariously from the comfort of a Lazy Boy recliner.

But what if God made you for more than a safe, routine, and boring life? What if you were created in his image to discover, to explore, and to live life on the edge?

I've discovered that most of our adventures can be experienced in everyday life. You can know adventure as you decide to be fully present and fully God's wherever you are and whatever you do.

- Parenting can be an adventure if you guide your children in becoming everything God wants them to be.
- Marriage can be an adventure if you choose to act as a student of your spouse no matter how long you've been married or how well you think you know each other.
- Friendship can be an adventure if you resolve to sharpen each other as iron sharpens iron.

Going to work, getting coffee at Starbucks, shopping at Costco, or taking a walk in your neighborhood can be an adventure if you see every encounter as a divine appointment and an opportunity to be like Jesus to the world around you.

Here's what I'm suggesting: attitude and perspective determine the measure of your exploits. You can aimlessly wander through life on cruise control or see every moment as a gift and live with God-inspired intentionality. That, my friends, is the key to living the adventure the Father has planned for you.

So tally-ho! Go for it! Adventure in the Kingdom is what you were made for.

What next?
Today, pray about starting your next adventure, be it big or small.

May I pray for you?
God, you didn't intend for us to lead boring lives. You've created adventures for each of us, and we want to experience them with full abandon! Get us off the couch and out into the world. Amen.

DAY 38: THE AGE OF ARROGANCE

"The eye cannot say to the hand, 'I don't need you!' And the head cannot say to the feet, 'I don't need you!' Now you are the body of Christ, and each one of you is a part of it" 1 Corinthians 12:21, 27.

Since the 1970s, computers and readily available digital data have transformed the way we think and function. If you want to know anything about everything, it's out there in cyberspace.

But is there a downside to being so data-rich? Have we assigned too much importance to our ability to find and disseminate knowledge? Here are five ponderings about the proliferation of information:

- When we put knowledge above wisdom and experience, we're being arrogant. I want to grow in knowledge, but knowledge without wisdom can lead to trouble. We need to understand how to apply knowledge (that's wisdom) and why it matters (that comes from experience).
- When talking trumps listening, we're being bigheaded. Part of the problem with everybody thinking they know more than the other guy is that we stop listening to each other. We form strong opinions based on the massive amount of data we digest on any particular subject. We believe we're experts, and

we really don't care what others know.

- When we're more concerned about being right than relational, we're being proud. When it's all said and done, God is not going to care about how much we knew (or thought we knew), but about how much we loved.

- When knowledge becomes our god, God and his Word seem irrelevant, and that's tragic. Many view the Bible as an extraneous book filled with myths and misinformation. The truth is, there is no other religious book that matches the wisdom, accuracy, knowledge, or credibility of the Bible.

- When the digital becomes dominant, we become independent rather than interdependent, and that's unwise. It's easier and more convenient to connect in cyberspace than in person. But we are made to live in community with others and to connect with real people in meaningful ways.

Grow in your knowledge. Experience the wonders of the digital age. But guard your heart and mind against an "age of arrogance" attitude that might cost you what matters most.

What next?
Today, give the Internet a rest and instead seek community and meaningful connection.

May I pray for you?

God, we are thankful for the Information Age! Please help us take advantage of the knowledge available without becoming arrogant in the process. Amen.

DAY 39: THE BLESSING OF PAIN

"Let us look only to Jesus, the one who began our faith and who makes it perfect. He suffered death on the cross. But he accepted the shame as if it were nothing because of the joy that God put before him…" Hebrews 12:2 NCV.

In his book, *The Problem of Pain,* C.S. Lewis wrote that we find pain troublesome "because our finite, human minds selfishly believe that pain-free lives would prove that God loves us." He goes on to say, "Love demands the perfecting of the beloved," because like gold, we are perfected in the fire of adversity.

Whether we like it or not, pain can be used to perfect us. We are, in fact, best molded into the image of God's Son through suffering. Even Jesus learned obedience through trials (see Hebrews 5:8).

We fight this reality. We can't imagine how a good and loving God could ever allow us to hurt. Some of us have turned our backs on God precisely because of the agony we've experienced. I did.

In my early 20s, I walked away from God for a season. I believed falsely that God existed to make me happy and healthy. I hadn't figured out yet that he's way more concerned about making me *holy*. As it happens, being holy leads to true happiness and spiritual and emotional health.

Of course I still pray for God's intervention and healing during struggles, but in the meantime, I want to develop a trust in God that is not contingent on my comfort or hinged on my happiness.

Perhaps, we need a different perspective on pain. Maybe the suffering we know, and even the suffering that comes through the sin of others against us, can be a tool in God's hand.

Maybe, just maybe, pain can become a blessing in your life.

What next?
Think of a time you suffered. In hindsight, can you see how God used the experience to benefit you?

May I pray for you?
Jesus, you know pain. You know betrayal and even death. But that wasn't the end of your story, and it doesn't have to be the end of ours. Hold us close. Heal our broken bodies and broken hearts. And in the meantime, help us look beyond the now to the joy that will be ours someday, either in this world or the next. Amen.

DAY 40: A GREAT MOM

"Her children arise and call her blessed; her husband also, and he praises her: 'Many women do noble things, but you surpass them all'" Proverbs 31:28-29.

My mom did her best, and she's always been a good mom, but I was prone to wander. I once got busted by my elementary principal for peeing on the boys' bathroom wall (I was writing my name). At the very same school, I was almost suspended for intentionally throwing a softball at the head of our playground monitor. And the list goes on....

My mother's ability to keep her head above the fray amazes me. She survived raising three boys and one girl (who I insist was spoiled), a marriage of twenty-plus years to a man who had his issues, and major moves to six states. She worked full-time, kept a busy house relatively sane, and as a pastor's wife, she put up with a thousand expectations of parishioners. Frankly, I don't know how she did it all.

So what makes a great mom great? Here are seven things I've noticed as a son, father and husband (married to another incredible mom):

- A great mom loves unconditionally. Her affection is not based on the performance of her children. Come hell or high water, good days or bad, she simply loves.

- A great mom says what she means and means what she says. You may not always like what she says, but you are rarely confused about her desires or intentions.
- A great mom disciplines, corrects, and molds her children with a view to their future. Her unconditional love does not mean unregulated tolerance for unruly behavior. She is committed to growth.
- A great mom provides the glue that keeps the family connected. She is the one who typically takes the initiative to gather the clan together for events.
- A great mom is a comforter. She seems to know what to say and when to say it to encourage and build up her kids. (And sometimes she doesn't say anything.)
- A great mom instills a sense of God-given purpose in the hearts and minds of her children. From an early age, they believe God has big plans for their lives.
- A great mom loves Jesus with all her heart, and she models faith and godliness to her children. They fall in love with Jesus because she is deeply in love with him.

Certainly, my list is far from complete, but I know each of these things mark the life of a great woman and mom.

What next?
Do you have a great mom? Call her today and express your love and appreciation.

May I pray for you?
God, thank you for moms! (They were a great idea!) May we treat them with the honor they deserve, and may we strive to become a parent who's blessed by our children. Amen.

DAY 41: AGE WITH GRACE

"The glory of the young is their strength; the gray hair of experience is the splendor of the old" Proverbs 20:29 NLT.

Recently, a friend recommended *Tuesdays with Morrie* by Mitch Albom. It's a moving and insightful book about an old professor (Morrie) who is dying of ALS, written by one of his former students (Mitch).

One of the chapters deals with the fear of aging. In it Morrie says, "…the young are not wise. They have very little understanding about life. I *embrace* aging. As you grow, you learn more. If you stayed at twenty-two, you'd always be as ignorant as you were at twenty-two. Aging is not just decay. It's growth. If you're always battling against getting older, you're always going to be unhappy because it will happen anyhow."

Busted. Again.

I'm pretty sure I haven't embraced aging, and I complain way too much about the decay and decline in my life. The symptoms of age are frustrating at times, but maybe I'm focusing on the wrong issues. Perhaps it would be better to settle here:

- I may not be able to do physically what I used to

do, but I've had the privilege of experiencing much in my life. I've climbed mountains, surfed oceans, trekked the Himalayas, run marathons, and thank God, I'm still moving.

- I might not sleep as much as I used to, but I sure do get a lot done at 5am!
- I've forgotten more than most twenty-somethings know, but wisdom does, in fact, make up for a lot.

Morrie is right, "Aging is not just decay. It's growth." Frankly, when I think about how idiotic I was in my youth, I'm eternally grateful for the maturity I've gained and for the spiritual development still to come.

What next?

Today, embrace aging. See it as a path that leads to an even better life forever with Jesus. Being older just means being closer to eternity.

May I pray for you?

Father, help us remember that though our bodies grow weaker, and our days on this earth are numbered, this life is not the be-all and end-all. Teach us to embrace each season of our existence with anticipation and joy. Amen.

DAY 42: LIFE LESSONS

"Man does not live on bread alone but on every word that comes from the mouth of the Lord" Deuteronomy 8:3.

Not long ago I engaged in a three-week fast inspired by the book of Daniel (see Daniel 1:12 and Daniel 10:2-3). I hate to fast, but I love the focus it gives me in my relationship with Jesus. Here are fifteen lessons I learned (or re-learned) during my experience:

1. God loves to reveal his majesty even in the messy moments of my life.
2. I can live without coffee (I think), but I can't live without love.
3. The single most important thing I need from God is not a thing…it is simply his presence.
4. Sometimes I measure life by a different set of standards than God does, and my standards are too often driven by broken cultural values.
5. Fame is fleeting. Only what I do for the honor of the Lord lasts forever.
6. There is a wretched little Pharisee in me who thinks too highly of himself and too little of others.
7. To change a culture you must change hearts. Hearts are changed through selfless acts of love, not through angry acts of rage.
8. Sometimes I ache for the brokenness of this world so much, yet I can't even begin to imagine the pain in

God's heart.

9. With God in the mix, the surreal becomes real; the impossible becomes HIMpossible.
10. I occasionally waste too much time worrying about the wrong things and focusing on the trivial rather than the eternal.
11. I must learn to live more for the Lord and less for the praise of others.
12. It's hard for me to teach the Word with anointing without first engaging my heart, mind, soul, and body in worship of the Anointed One.
13. Life is precious. Life is hard. And life is often lived in tension between those two realities.
14. God loves to create the extraordinary out of the ordinary; it makes him smile.
15. To live without the possibility of loss is to live without the potential of adventure. To eliminate risk is to eliminate the prospect of great joy.

What next?

Pick a time to fast this week and then write down your insights from the experience.

May I pray for you?

God, our society distracts us with values and desires that are not eternal. Speak to the hearts of those who choose to fast this week, and refocus their minds on you. And may those who aren't able to fast instead benefit from the lessons I learned. Amen.

DAY 43: THE CASE FOR CHURCH

"How good and pleasant it is when God's people live together in unity!" Psalm 133:1.

It seems the trend nowadays is to treat church attendance as no big deal. For many, going is a secondary option if they don't have anything better to do.

I've heard all the reasons for considering church optional: *It's my only day off. There are too many hypocrites in the church. Church is boring. All they talk about is money. I've had some bad experiences. I don't need to go to church to love and follow Christ.*

Do any of these statements sound familiar to you? Here are eight compelling answers that address the question, "Why should I go to church?"

1. It is biblical. Hebrews 10:25, "Let us not give up meeting together as some have." The biblical pattern is regular attendance and meaningful connection with the Church.
2. It can help prevent falling away from the faith. Through regular fellowship, we are encouraged to remain steadfast and devoted (1 Thess. 5:11).
3. It provides spiritual community. "They devoted themselves to the apostles' teaching and to the fellowship, to the breaking of bread and to prayer"

(Acts 2:42). These are communal activities that happen in connection with real people.

4. It supports the Great Commandment. Matthew 12:30, "Love the Lord your God with all your heart and with all your soul and with all your mind and with all your strength." To love God is to love what he loves, and he loves his bride, the Church!

5. It follows Jesus's own example. We see a pattern in Christ's life of going to the place of public worship. If Jesus were walking on planet earth today, we would find him in church on Sunday. If you are a Christ-follower, follow him and do the same.

6. It provides you important instruction from the Word of God. Being instructed by and challenged through God's Word helps bring spiritual maturity to your life.

7. It gives you a practical and regular place to serve others. 1 Corinthians chapters 12 and 14 show the importance of each Christian using their spiritual gifts. Church is not the only place to serve, but it is an important one.

8. Finally, it is good to hang together. Unity takes practice and doesn't get developed when we are spiritual hermits or too selective in our relationships.

Trust me, I know the Church and its leaders (like me) are far from perfect. But the Body of Christ is the Bride of Jesus. He loves his bride and wants us to love her as well.

What next?

If you don't attend church regularly, make a commitment to go faithfully for the next six months and see what happens.

May I pray for you?

God, you intend for us to do life together. Unify us as one body, your Bride, and bless our efforts as we seek you faithfully in community. We can do more together than we can alone. Amen.

DAY 44: THE WEIGHT OF WAITING

"The steps of the godly are directed by the Lord. He delights in every detail of their lives" Psalm 37:23.

The nurse did what nurses do; she put me in a room, told me to strip down to my skivvies, don the breezy hospital gown, and wait for the doc.

Forty minutes later the nurse entered my room with another patient. She was shocked to see me there. "Oh, I'm so sorry. I thought the doctor was through with you. We must have gotten our wires crossed." You've got to be kidding me.

I hate waiting. I despise wasting time. I know patience is a virtue, but I'm pretty sure it's one I may never master. Maybe you can relate….

Maybe you've been waiting for that new job or a raise for a long time. Maybe you've been waiting for years for Mr. or Mrs. Right to come along and sweep you off your feet. Maybe God gave you a promise long ago, and it's becoming harder and harder to hold on to that promise.

Waiting is hard. I know. But Psalm 37 offers wisdom for dealing with the weight of waiting:

- Don't worry (verse 1). Rather than fret, stew, and

worry—we wait and trust.
- Don't envy (verse 1). Rather than lose our focus in desire for something or someone—we seek God above all else.
- Take delight in the Lord (verse 4). Rather than feel anxious—we're still in his presence.
- Commit everything you do to the Lord (verse 5). Rather than take matters into our own hands—we entrust our lives to him and believe in his plan.
- Wait patiently for God to act (verse 7). Rather than force something—we commit everything to his care.
- Turn from your rage (verse 8). Rather than fume when we don't get our way—we fix our eyes and heart on God and experience his peace.

Like I said, I'm not a great wait-er, but I'm starting to understand that waiting can be good for me because it's working on my character. (Maybe waiting isn't a waste of time after all.) Perhaps, the next time I find myself in a holding pattern, I will see it as an opportunity to grow in Jesus.

Possibly, you will too.

What next?
What has God taught you in your seasons of waiting? Write down your insights and refer to them next time you feel the weight of waiting.

May I pray for you?

God, may we, despite the distressing struggle of waiting, find you at our side directing our steps even when we can't see it. Please comfort us as we wait, knowing that you delight in every detail of our lives. Amen.

DAY 45: OVERCOMING CYNICISM

"Finally, brothers and sisters, whatever is true, whatever is noble, whatever is right, whatever is pure, whatever is lovely, whatever is admirable—if anything is excellent or praiseworthy—think about such things" Philippians 4:8.

The older I get the easier it is to be a negative and disparaging skeptic. Sometimes I'm like the old fart who shuffles along in the grocery store complaining out loud to himself about people, prices, and politicians.

It seems fashionable to criticize just about everything and everyone. We have become a nation of people quick to throw stones at others for their failures while conveniently ignoring our own.

You see, life is hard. Things go left when we want them to go right. People let us down. Dreams are shattered. Plans sometimes fail. Friends betray us. What's more, our own bodies let us down.

If we're not careful, it's easy to become pessimistic and grumpy. It's easy to see the worst in people rather than believe the best. It's too easy to give up and just wallow in our misery.

But there's a better way:

- Decide to guard your heart, and ask God to help you stay tender despite the emotional beatings you sometimes experience at the hand of others.
- Do whatever it takes to find the best in your circumstances and in people.
- Remember that you too are far from perfect and still in the process of becoming the man or woman God wants you to be.
- Get off your high horse of spiritual or intellectual superiority and be humble.

I want to grow in grace with age. I choose to see past the pain that could lead to cynicism and instead fix my eyes on the eternal. Rather than become a snarky old saint, I pray to become more like Jesus.

What next?

Examine the state of your heart. Are you growing cynical? Reread the verse above and choose to focus on the eternal.

May I pray for you?

God, you fashioned the earth and everything in it, and you made us for a purpose. Please don't allow us to lose sight of your will and creation. Focus our attention on what is true, right and pure, and equip us to be lights that shine in the darkness. Amen.

DAY 46: BROKENNESS

"This High Priest of ours understands our weaknesses, for he faced all of the same testings we do, yet he did not sin. So let us come boldly to the throne of our gracious God. There we will receive his mercy, and we will find grace to help us when we need it most" Hebrews 4:15-16 NLT.

We've all sinned and will continue to sin on this side of eternity. Parts of our hearts, minds, souls, and bodies contain imperfections. Thankfully, the day is coming when God will refine us and make us whole. But I'm not that person yet (and neither are you).

A while back, I spoke with a young Christian man who struggles with pornography. Consumed by guilt, he felt disqualified to serve God because of his sin. His life lacked joy, and he wanted to walk away from his faith because he believed Jesus was disgusted with him.

Does Jesus care about your sin? Absolutely. Does it matter when you're bound by unholy and unhealthy habits? Oh yeah. Are there consequences for your poor choices? Often.

The answer isn't to give in to sinful impulses without concern (abusing the gift of grace) or to quit your walk with God (abandoning grace). He understands you. He knows your human condition. He recognizes the spiritual war you face every day.

However, here's why your brokenness should encourage you:

- It's the messed up that discover God in the middle of their mess.
- It's the weak that find God's strength.
- It's the sinful that recognize their need for mercy and grace.
- It's the needy person who empathizes with other beggars standing in line.
- It's the sick and broken that realize they need help.
- It's the humble person who forgives as they have been forgiven.

Regardless of your particular pattern of failure, remedy it by running to God's throne of mercy and grace. Say *yes* to God, and *no* to sin, more often than not. Maybe God expects you to struggle more than you do.

What next?
If you wrestle with poor choices and habits, ask the Lord for help today.

May I pray for you?
Father, sometimes we do well, and sometimes we don't. Help us remember that you are faithful, merciful, and full of grace even when we are not. Teach us to draw near to you no matter how messed up and broken we are, for you are the healer and redeemer we so desperately need. Amen.

DAY 47: CHILDLIKE FAITH

"Let the smile of your face shine on us, O Lord" Psalm 4:6.

People worry about getting old. Americans spend billions of dollars every year doing whatever it takes to look younger. We primp, pluck, nip and tuck in a futile attempt to avoid the inevitable.

I'm all for staying in shape and practicing healthy grooming, but the fact is, we're all aging. Wrinkles, aches, pains, and cracks will come; it's just a matter of time.

That being said, what we *can* continue to enhance is our childlike faith. No matter our physical age, our hearts and our confidence in God can always grow younger.

God delights over me as a dad delights over his children! When he gazes at me, he smiles. He doesn't just see a broken body. He doesn't see my sordid past or my imperfect present. He knows my weaknesses. He knows everything about me. But when he looks at me, he looks at me with the love and delight of a father.

The question is: when I look at him, what do I see? Do I see delight in his eyes? Do I see joy in his heart for me? Do I peer through the eyes of a child?

- When I leap, do I believe he will catch me?
- When I cry out, do I know he will come to my aid?
- When I hurt, do I believe he will comfort me?
- When I fear, do I know he will protect me?
- When I falter, do I believe he will pick me up?
- When I lack, do I know he will provide for me?
- When I lose my way, do I believe he will find me?
- When I fail, do I know he will always love me no matter what?

I can't do much about my rusting old shell of a body, but I can give my faith a facelift. Maybe I should focus more on my childlike hope in the one who is, and always will be, my heavenly Father. He is a father who would do *anything* for you and me because he loves us beyond our wildest imaginings.

What next?
Take a moment to answer the questions above. If you answer *no* to any, ask God for a heart makeover.

May I pray for you?
Lord, as we grow older, may our faith remain young and energetic. Let your smile shine on us, God, as we pursue you with childlike determination, believing your promises and desiring to please you above all else. Amen.

DAY 48: THE LITTLE THINGS

"Who is wise and understanding among you? Let them show it by their good life, by deeds done in the humility that comes from wisdom" James 3:13.

If you don't think small things matter, you've probably never slept in a room with a mosquito. Certainly, we often give too much credence to minor issues, but just as often we ignore important little things that deserve our attention.

For example, the fact that I'm a slob who drops his socks on the floor in front of the dirty clothes hamper (rather than inside it) might not matter at first. However, after the 100th time it becomes a big deal to my wife.

One small ding on my car door from a careless person in the parking lot is just one tiny blemish, nothing to fret about. But a hundred dings become a noticeable dent.

When it comes to acts of kindness toward my wife, she always appreciates the big things I do for her, but she deeply values the many little things too. Opening the door for her. Holding her hand in public. Calling her from the office at least once a day just to say, "I love you."

So how do you know what really matters? When are the little things truly no big deal and when are they potentially a very big deal?

Here are some ways to measure what is important:

- Ask and listen. When in doubt, ask your spouse or friend, "Does this matter to you?"
- Be a good fruit inspector. Take time to honestly evaluate the fruit (i.e. results) of your actions.
- Does it matter to you? If so, it probably matters to others around you. The biblical mandate is to treat others the way you want to be treated (Luke 6:31).
- Did the stockpiling of what you thought were small issues lead to some serious conflict?
- Has the ignoring of little things resulted in desensitization on your part toward sin or the feelings of others?

What next?
Today, look for small acts of kindness you can do to bless your family and friends.

May I pray for you?
Jesus, you performed many major miracles, but you also enacted smaller ones to show love to those close to you. We don't want to forget that little things matter. Please help us to practice "deeds done in humility" in order to bless our family and friends. Amen.

DAY 49: ARE YOU A LOSER TOO?

"Whoever finds their life will lose it, and whoever loses their life for my sake will find it" Matthew 10:39.

True confession: a while back I bought a *Mega Millions* lotto ticket. I'm a little embarrassed to admit that. I marched into Chester Store and asked (somewhat sheepishly) for numbers 06, 31, 33, 60, 74, and 05.

Next thing I knew, I was walking out of the store with my winning ticket! I felt giddy all day. What if I won? I mean, somebody was going to win, so why not me?

I'd tithe.

I'd give extra to my favorite charities.

When interviewed on thousands of television stations worldwide, I would give God all the credit. He'd be the hero of this story.

That night I logged on to the *Mega Millions* website. My hands shook in anticipation.

Wait, those aren't my numbers! Why wouldn't God let a nice guy like me win?

Then a few things dawned on me....

- I probably wasn't the only person praying for a winning ticket.
- I don't need money to be happy.
- In God's economy, the way to win is to lose.

Maybe life—true life—and joy don't come from the things we think they come from. Maybe the path to winning and living is losing and dying.

How about you? Where are you looking for life? Remember, it's only truly found in Him.

What next?
Today, find a way to be a "loser." Put someone else's needs or desires above your own.

May I pray for you?
God, our world wars against this counter-cultural teaching. Thank you for your example on the cross. Help us overcome our society's expectations for success. Amen.

DAY 50: HANDLING CRITICISM

"Words can bring death or life" Proverbs 18:21.

Some time ago after a service, a woman walked up to me with fire in her eyes. She looked ticked, and I was about to become the brunt of her unrestrained wrath.

"I am so fed up with you preachers telling me to trust Jesus," she said. "You have *no* idea what it's like to have two teenage kids who are always in trouble! You have *no* idea what it's like to live with a worthless man who sucks the life out of you! You have *no* idea what it's like to wish you could hit the 'do over' button!" Then, after emotionally puking all over me, she turned and stomped away in disgust.

I thought about going after her, but she scared me, and I was more than a little dumbfounded by her reaction to what I thought was a great message on trust. Silly me.

Her harsh words sent me into a nosedive. I knew at that moment I could choose to lie in a cesspool of self-analyzing misery or put into practice some tactics I've learned about handling criticism and rejection:

- Respond rather than react. In fact, intentionally under-react.
- Evaluate honestly, "What can I learn through this?"

Cut yourself some slack here too; you're not as good or perfect as you'd like. It's okay.
- Remember, often we speak to others out of our pain and frustration. People fail just like we fail! Aspire to understand the offender.
- Try not to take everything so personally. It might not be about you.
- Take your pain to Jesus. He handles it best.
- Try to listen first and foremost to the voice that matters most. Sometimes we need to turn down the volume of our critics and turn up our sensitivity to the Father's words.
- Forgive as you've been forgiven. Holding on to our desire for retribution or revenge is not an option.

Have you ever been the brunt of someone's disparaging remarks? I've come to understand and accept that criticism is unavoidable. We must learn to keep our eyes on Jesus who was criticized too.

What next?
Next time you feel hurt by someone's harsh words, ask the Lord to help you grow through the experience. Use the above strategy to assist in the process.

May I pray for you?
God, help us cling to your loving truth when faced with the animosity of others. Instill in our hearts the sense of intrinsic value that comes from being your child. Amen.

DAY 51: LESSONS FROM FROG AND TOAD

"From now on, brothers and sisters, if anything is excellent and if anything is admirable, focus your thoughts on these things: all that is true, all that is holy, all that is just, all that is pure, all that is lovely, and all that is worthy of praise" Philippians 4:8 CEB.

For decades I've read to my children, and now grandchildren, the fun adventures of *Frog and Toad*. These children's books, written by Arnold Lobel, are some of my favorites.

Frog is taller, friendlier and much more positive than Toad. Toad is shorter and the more serious and anxious of the two. Their humorous escapades include some wonderful lessons for children and adults.

For Toad, the glass is not half-empty or half-full—it's just dirty. Even acts of kindness (like attempting to bring Frog some ice cream), usually end up in a mess or a disaster of some sort.

Frog is kinder and wiser. He sees the best in life and the best in his friend. Frog continually takes on the role of encourager even though his grouchy buddy often rebuffs his efforts.

Toad is such a toad.

What have I learned from these two?

- It's better to be a frog (positive) than a toad (negative).
- Attitude affects everything.
- Life rarely goes the way we want or expect.
- For those who have eyes to see, adventures are everywhere.
- Friendship is costly and priceless.

The other day, while reading a chapter to my grandson, Caleb, I started to wonder, "Is life really that simple? Can most of the world be described as toad-like or frog-like?"

I'm still pondering that question, but here's my deep philosophical and spiritual insight for the day: I'd rather be a builder than a destroyer, an encourager than a discourager, and much more of a frog than a toad.

What next?
Are you a frog or a toad? Today, choose to be a frog and see how people react.

May I pray for you?
God, the world is full of toads! Yet in your Word you ask us to be encouragers, to appreciate all that is lovely, and to serve with joyful hearts. Help us to be frogs! Amen.

DAY 52: MAKE TODAY GREAT!

"I'd say you'll do best by filling your minds and meditating on things true, noble, reputable, authentic, compelling, gracious—the best, not the worst; the beautiful, not the ugly; things to praise, not things to curse. Put into practice what you learned from me, what you heard and saw and realized. Do that, and God, who makes everything work together, will work you into his most excellent harmonies" Philippians 4:8-9 TM.

We typically define a good day based on how life is going or how we feel. So if circumstances are tough, we say our day is bad. If the kids drove us crazy, the day was hard. If the dog ate the couch or the car bit the dust, it was horrible.

What's more, whether our mood is good or bad also determines the goodness or badness of our day. Life is tough sometimes. For some, life is difficult all the time.

Here's the question: is it possible to have a good day despite not-so-good experiences and circumstances? Here are some ways to make a bad day great:

- Focus on the *Who* more than the *what*. Keep your eyes on God no matter what and he'll give you perspective. No problem we face is eternal, only God is. No situation is without end. God is forever.

Nothing you face is beyond him, a surprise to him, or bigger than him. Fix your heart on Jesus. It's amazing how this simple step brings clarity and peace.

- Choose to believe that something bigger and better can happen *in* you despite the challenges *around* you. Do you believe that God is at work in your life? Do you believe that he is good even when life is bad? Will you choose to believe that he is able to redeem, restore, and renew anything surrendered to him?

- Make up your mind to be thankful *in* all things even when you aren't thankful *for* all things. I know the power of thankfulness. Not only am I suggesting we choose to believe God is always at work in our lives, but I'm advocating thankfulness as a way of life.

- Make the choice to *affect* your environment, not just *reflect* it. Don't get moody, blue, grumpy and ugly when your world gets cold; instead, do or say something that brings godly and positive change.

What next?

Go ahead, I double-dog-dare you to give these four steps a try for the next 24 hours and see what happens!

May I pray for you?

God, may we meditate on you and focus our minds and hearts on what is pure, faultless and right. Even when our circumstances threaten to crush us, we know we can trust you to work for our benefit. Thank you for taking care of us, for teaching us, and for loving us. Amen.

DAY 53: AVOIDING BURNOUT

"Remember the Sabbath day by keeping it holy" Exodus 20:8.

As boys, my sons used to watch a Saturday morning cartoon called *Teenage Mutant Ninja Turtles* (TMNT). My youngest, Isaac, was enthralled with TMNT. In fact, after almost every program he would "go ninja" on his siblings. I once tried to explain to him, "Isaac, turtles are not really violent, and they don't move like lightning or eat pizza." His reply was classic, "Dad, they're mutants, of course they do!"

Sadly, in our culture, we tend to make heroes out of mutants. We think the multi-millionaire executive who works eighty hours a week is a stud. We admire the politician or pastor who sacrifices all for the sake of the masses. We envy the Grammy-winning performer who lives out of a suitcase as he or she travels the globe.

But let's hit the way-back button and take a look at something God implemented thousands of years ago after he set his people free from bondage in Egypt. It's called the Sabbath, and it's the fourth of the Ten Commandments.

The word used in the Old Testament is *shabath*, and it means "to intercept or interrupt." The term implies a complete cessation of regular activity. Sabbath is the one day when your work is done, even if it isn't.

The concept is ancient, but for many the practice is forgotten or ignored. It's a simple idea to understand but difficult to apply. However, when you choose a crazy life, you lose perspective. You find it impossible to know peace. Without margin you experience little joy, because delight is found in the quiet places of your soul during moments of reflection and rest.

We often feel overwhelmed with all the noise and activity on planet earth. Tragically, we try to cram as much as we can into every moment of every day, but our over-productivity becomes counterproductive.

The abundant life Jesus wants for us is epic, but not insane. It is full, but not stuffed. In fact, Jesus said, "Come to me, all you who are weary and burdened, and I will give you rest" (Matthew 11:28). Sabbath. Margin. Rest. This is the pathway to a truly holy and healthy existence.

What next?
Do you practice a regular Sabbath? If not, make it a habit for the next four weeks.

May I pray for you?
God, we can trace the concept of Sabbath to the creation of earth. If it was important to you, it should be important to us too. Help us keep the Sabbath holy. Amen.

DAY 54: BEING THANKFUL

"Let the peace that Christ gives control your thinking, because you were all called together in one body to have peace. Always be thankful" Colossians 3:15 NCV.

A while ago I read *One Thousand Gifts* by Ann Voskamp. The book inspired me to create my own list of gratitude. And while I could easily fill a hundred pages with everything I thank God for, here's a short list:

- Rain that washes and refreshes.
- Swallows that seem to really enjoy what they do.
- Children and grandchildren who make me smile (and sometimes cry).
- My church; filled with people I love.
- Cashews (I just ate a handful).
- My amazing wife (who loves me even when I'm a handful).
- Moments of silence in my busy world.
- God's provision from the most unexpected places at times.
- The song I keep singing/whistling: *Come As You Are* by Pocket Full of Rocks.
- Friends who take the time to read my musings.

How about you? Do you appreciate the gifts God has lavished upon you, or do you dwell on the difficulties and disappointments of life instead? (For the record, sometimes difficulties and disappointments morph into unexpected blessings!)

Whatever your current situation holds, an attitude of gratitude will serve you far better than resentment and anger ever could. Choose to be thankful!

What next?

Today, make a list of at least 10 things you thank God for. They don't have to be big things or even spiritual things. Your list might include hard circumstances that you have decided to be thankful for rather than bitter about. So grab a pen, quiet your heart, and start writing.

May I pray for you?

God, we have more to appreciate than not! Sometimes we get caught up in negativity and pessimism, but you call us to be joyful and content. Lord, fill our hearts with gratitude, and supply us with a peace that surpasses all understanding. Amen.

DAY 55: DEALING WITH DEATH

"Teach us to number our days, that we may gain a heart of wisdom" Psalm 90:12.

Dealing with death is emotionally difficult and sobering. But the reality of our mortality isn't anything to fear. Rather, we must face it. We're all stamped with an expiration date. Not one of us owns our next breath.

When my wife and I celebrated our 38th wedding anniversary in 2013, we talked about the fact it's highly unlikely we'll share another thirty-eight years together on planet earth. Sad but true.

So here are some wise lessons I'm learning about finishing well:

- Don't waste the gift of time. We all have the same twenty-four hours in a day. What you do with yours, however, is up to you. Are you living on purpose? Do you see each minute as a gift from God?
- Keep short accounts. By that, I mean don't let the sun go down on your anger (Ephesians 4:26). People are too precious to cut out of your life in frustration and wrath. Here's a little insight: we all fail. Sooner or later the people you love will hurt you (and you will hurt them). Love and forgive anyhow.
- Live with honor; die with honor. Basically, this means

you do everything possible to finish well. Make it your goal to live honorably for Jesus every day so when the time comes for your departure, you can say with Paul, "I have fought the good fight, I have finished the race, I have kept the faith" (2 Timothy 4:7).

With modern medicine and a relatively healthy lifestyle, I might make it to a hundred. More than likely, however, I'm already well past the halfway mark, and that's okay. I'm more aware than ever that I am one day closer to eternity, and that's a good thing. It inspires me to live in such a way that makes every moment count.

Are you ready to go home when the Lord calls? Are you ready to be reunited with your family and friends who have gone on before you? Are you ready for an eternity with Jesus?

What next?
If you knew your life would end in the next twenty-four hours, how would you spend your remaining time? Did you discover potential regrets in your answer? Take steps today to ensure you exit this life well.

May I pray for you?
God, our days are numbered, and you numbered them! Help us live life to the fullest with our eyes heavenward, seeking you with all our hearts. Amen.

DAY 56: LESSONS LEARNED AT 37,000 FEET

"Now you've got my feet on the life path, all radiant from the shining of your face. Ever since you took my hand, I'm on the right way" Psalm 16:11 TM.

A while ago I flew to San Diego for a conference. After squeezing into the dreaded middle seat and checking to make sure there was an airsick bag (I'm prone to motion sickness), I said *hi* to the fellow inmates on either side of me. They pretty much pretended I didn't exist. Inspired by the experiences flying offers, I pulled out my iPad and took some notes.

- Many live isolated lives. We want our personal space, and we're not really interested in the other guy's story. The new normal is to live in our little bubbles and keep to ourselves. But wouldn't it be better to share even a piece of our lives? No man is an island (especially in the middle seat).
- Life is bumpy at times. I religiously search for the infamous chuck bag every time I get on a plane. I don't want to be caught unprepared. I expect the unexpected, and I plan ahead for what might happen. Maybe that's not a bad way to live life too.
- You can't live long on snacks. The micro-bag of airline pretzels isn't meant to truly satisfy. Some try

to live their spiritual life on spiritual snacks too. They get just a little Word here and a little prayer there, but not nearly enough to thrive.

- Location matters. On a flight, our location affects our view and comfort. In our spiritual life, location also matters. The Bible says in Colossians 3:1, "Since, then, you have been raised with Christ, set your hearts on things above, where Christ is, seated at the right hand of God."

- There are lots of things we don't adequately appreciate. One good aspect of flying is it reminds me of the benefits on the ground that I take for granted! Truth is I am blessed.

- We all have baggage. Whether it's an actual suitcase or emotional wounds and relational issues, we often carry heavy burdens. Maybe it's time to get rid of some baggage and check it with Jesus.

- Travel is necessary to get to another location. As much as I dislike air travel nowadays, flying is often the best transportation. You can't escape travel in life, either; it requires motion. I can't grow or change without it. First, I need a destination; then I need to move.

What next?

Whether you take the road less traveled, or a jumbo jet, make time to reflect on your life today.

May I pray for you?

God, as we journey through this life (in anticipation of the next!) may we travel well, with you as our ever-present companion. Amen.

DAY 57: CHRISTIANS ARE WEIRD

"The human body has many parts, but the many parts make up one whole body. So it is with the body of Christ. Some of us are Jews, some are Gentiles, some are slaves, and some are free. But we have all been baptized into one body by one Spirit, and we all share the same Spirit" 1 Corinthians 12:12-13 NLT.

I love the Bride of Jesus, but after more than 50 years of church experience, trust me when I say the Bride is weird.

By *weird* I don't mean crazy-uncle-Bob weird, I simply mean peculiar-and-unusual weird. The Church consists of every tribe, nation, social-economic, and political group on the planet. If that doesn't make the church odd and unique, then what does?

Furthermore, within the Church, there is a vast assortment of biblical perspectives, historical traditions, and experiential distinctiveness that each faction guards with zeal. We tend to hold on to our pet doctrines with a vengeance.

So how should we view our differences?

- I think our differences can be an asset in the hands of God.
- I think there is variety in the Body of Christ, and

that's a good thing because there are all kinds of people on the planet.

- I think we can hold dearly to our particular beliefs and pet doctrines without standing in condescension and judgment of others who will be with us forever in eternity.
- I think we should worry less about compromise and more about compassion.
- I think we can practice unity without the mistaken belief of Unitarianism.
- I think a good Catholic brother named Augustine got it right, "In essentials, unity; in non-essentials, liberty; in all things, charity."

What are the *essentials*? Here they are in one passage:

"For what I received I passed on to you as of first importance: that Christ died for our sins according to the Scriptures, that he was buried, and that he was raised on the third day according to the Scriptures" 1 Corinthians 15:3-4.

What matters most? Simply Jesus, dying for our sins. Nothing else is of equal value.

What next?
Embrace your weirdness and use it to point people to Jesus, the one who unites us.

May I pray for you?

God, thank you for our differences! Help us focus more on you and less on us. Amen.

DAY 58: WORDS MATTER

"The soothing tongue is a tree of life, but a perverse tongue crushes the spirit" Proverbs 15:4.

Ron managed the grocery store where I worked during high school. Typically, I stocked shelves from 4am to 8am, Monday through Thursday, and I'd arrive at midnight on Friday to put in an eight-hour shift. How I graduated with a 3.6 GPA is a mystery.

Tough guy Ron came from the old school of lion-like management, believing that intimidation increased productivity. I'm not sure if his vocabulary included *any* kind words, but if so, he never used them on me. Although I forgave Ron decades ago, his critical remarks haunt my memory to this day.

Why is it so easy to be negative? Why do we say hurtful things so often? We know, from firsthand experience, that sticks and stones may break our bones, but words *do*, in fact, also break us, and yet we say them anyhow.

I fear that in a culture that values sarcasm and devalues self-control we have become masters of cutting people to shreds with our tongue.

- We put someone else down to lift ourselves up (or so we hope).

- We believe it's funny to leave someone speechless with our witty retort.
- We have drifted from healthy debate and constructive criticism to degrading and verbal ugliness.

How would life change if instead of pain, our words brought healing? What if we were known for "encouraging and building others up" (1 Thessalonians 5:11)?

There's a place for truth-telling if we need correction, but it is always to be truth spoken *in love*. The Apostle Paul wrote, "If I speak in the tongues of men or of angels, but do not have love, I am only a resounding gong or a clanging cymbal. Love is patient, love is kind. It does not envy, it does not boast, it is not proud. It does not dishonor others, it is not self-seeking, it is not easily angered, it keeps no record of wrongs. Love…always protects, always trusts, always hopes, always perseveres" (1 Corinthians 13:1, 4-6).

What next?
Today, make a conscious effort to build up those around you by using encouraging words.

May I pray for you?

God, help us guard both our hearts and our mouths. Reveal the source of negativity in our minds, and renew our thoughts and the words that flow from them to others. Teach us to speak the language of love. In a world filled with hate and destruction, help us become beacons of light that heal. Amen.

DAY 59: COLLECTING ANTIQUES

"No one pours new wine into old leather wineskins; otherwise, the wine would burst the wineskins and the wine would be lost and the wineskins destroyed. But new wine is for new wineskins" Mark 2:22 CEB.

When it comes to really old stuff, there are two kinds of people, those who love antiques and those who don't. Which are you?

Antiques are cool (guess you know which group I'm in), but they're still just temporary things destined for destruction. God is more into the new. It's not that the old is evil, but just because it's old doesn't make it sacred.

The religious men of Jesus's time believed their spiritual practices and traditions were above all. Regular fasting (with an audience) and all of their Sabbath customs mattered more to them than truly loving God and people.

God always puts people first. Rather than objects or customs or traditions, being fresh and fully alive matters more to him, and evidently the Father loves the new.

Paul wrote, "…if anyone is in Christ, that person is part of the *new* creation. The old things have gone away, and look, *new* things have arrived!" 2 Corinthians 5:17 (CEB, emphasis added).

Let's be honest, some of us hold on to our old ways, our traditions, and the familiar with a death grip. We get terribly frustrated when something we hold dear is altered.

Maybe there's nothing wrong with the old, and it's good to be stretched by the new. Maybe we should zoom out and see the bigger picture. Is the new way more effective? Does the new approach connect better with our rapidly changing culture? Is there really anything wrong with new and different rather than old and familiar?

I'd rather grow old and stay flexible than grow old and become rigid. There's something inherent in the new that keeps me humble and dependent on God.

What next?
Ask God to keep your heart fresh and help you embrace the new with a better attitude. Determine to renew your mind daily so that his new wine has room to expand in your life. New might be hard, but if it helps us become more like Jesus, it's good.

May I pray for you?
God, help us accept new challenges, new opportunities, and "new wine." Rather than fight for our comfort zone, we want to follow a creative Creator who constantly calls us to something fresh, something innovative, and something new. Amen.

DAY 60: DEAD EYES

"The eye is the light of the body. When your eye is good, your whole body is full of light. When your eye is sinful, your whole body is full of darkness" Luke 11:34 NLV.

At the end of a recent trip to southern California, my wife and I stopped in Venice Beach for a cup of java before our flight home. The place was packed. I hate to stereotype people, but most of the individuals in line fit the bill of California weird. Like a prom queen in a biker bar, I felt out of sorts in this strange place.

Two women especially caught my attention. One black, the other white, both in their twenties, and beautiful. We only shared a spot in line for about five minutes, but those two will share a place in my heart for a long time. And it's not because they were gorgeous; it's because they seemed so lost.

They had hot bodies but dead eyes.

Despite their attractiveness and attire, what struck me most was the hopelessness in their eyes. You've heard it said, "The eyes are the window to the soul." In fact, scientists discovered that patterns in the iris can give an indication of whether we are warm and trusting or neurotic and impulsive. Simply put, our eyes tell all.

A life filled with spiritual darkness, versus a godly life, is reflected in the eyes. In fact, when people are filled with the light of God, it affects their entire being. Conversely, a broken life of moral decadence is also projected.

I'm not judging these women or claiming to know anything about their lives, but the image of these two still haunts me.

All around us are people who look pretty on the outside, but they are desperate for hope, freedom, joy, and real life. In fact, sometimes the ones who look the best are hurting the worst.

What do your eyes say about you? When you look at others, what do you see?

What next?
Today, try to see people as the Lord sees them. Pray that Jesus will break your heart with the things that break his.

May I pray for you?
Father, give us ears to hear and eyes to see. Give us your heart for the billions lost in darkness. Driven by compassion, as Jesus was, give us boldness to be beacons of grace to a world bound by gloom. Amen.

DAY 61: IN A FOG

"No eye has seen, no ear has heard, and no mind has imagined what God has prepared for those who love him" 1 Corinthians 2:9 NLT.

Some time ago, with a cup of coffee in my hand, I sat in my favorite chair looking out toward the hills behind my house. I love the view.

As I drank my java, a cold, wet fog began to roll in, and my beautiful view quickly deteriorated into a white mass of nothing. It happens. I live in the Northwest, and the weather can change pretty rapidly and dramatically.

Here's what struck me: the hills in all their splendor were still there, only my view of them had changed.

Life is that way. We humans, at best, have a three-dimensional ability to see the world around us. Our vision is limited. It is restricted by our humanness on the one hand and by circumstances beyond our control on the other.

When a cold, miserable, and blinding fog enters into your world, it is hard to see beyond the pain. It is hard to trust that God is good. It is hard to get past your agony, your loss, and your overwhelming sorrow. It feels a lot like you have been blindfolded and told to walk along the edge of the Grand Canyon. It's scary. It can be hard to keep walking when you fear plunging to your death with a single wrong step into a chasm of darkness below.

Fog happens.

But imagine with me a different way to live. Imagine what our lives might be like if we trust the one who has no limitations and no vision restrictions. God sees the beginning from the end. Time is not linear to him; it's eternal. How might your life be radically different if you accepted the blindfold and then walked along the edge of the cliff knowing that he is the one holding your hand and guiding your path?

God has a plan that goes beyond our ability to figure it out. Maybe he is up to something we can't see yet. Truth is, on this side of eternity, we may never understand it all, but maybe this side of eternity is just that—only a blip on the radar screen in the grand scale of all things eternal.

So hold on. Stay the course. Trust God. He has a plan (even when we can't see it).

What next?

Are you experiencing a "fog" right now? Trust the Lord to walk you through it.

May I pray for you?

God, we don't always know where you're leading us, but we can trust you regardless. Help us, and increase our faith when we can't see what's ahead. Amen.

DAY 62: PURSUING EXCELLENCE

"People were overwhelmed with amazement. 'He has done everything well,' they said" Mark 7:37.

We live in a world that values excellence. For the most part, what we view on primetime television, see in a theater, or experience at our favorite theme park is highly produced and polished. We expect nothing less.

Within the Church, this presents us with serious challenges. People don't anticipate (or want) Hollywood when they walk through the doors, but they do expect quality.

So should the Church pursue excellence? How can we do so without compromising our spiritual values? And how can we do our best without struggling under the burden of perfectionism on the one hand and people-pleasing on the other?

Here's my take:

- Our heart's desire is to honor God who deserves our very best. It's not about being perfect; it's about esteeming the Perfect One.
- Our goal is to remove distractions. We want to get out of the way and point people to Jesus. But if they can't get past the out-of-tune guitar or the out-of-touch teacher, we've created barriers, not bridges. Jesus

pointed people to God, and that's our motivation for pursuing excellence.

- Our attitude is humble and grateful regardless of the eventual outcome. Frankly, even when we've done our best to prepare, sometimes the unexpected happens. When it does, we never destroy any singer, drama team member, or volunteer through harsh criticism. We grow. We learn. We keep trying to improve while humbly acknowledging that our best efforts will fall short at times.

- Our focus is on faithfulness, not fickleness. We won't change things for the sake of change, but as faithful stewards of Kingdom gifts and resources, we will improve whatever needs improvement.

- Our end game is to bless God and to bless people. We don't expect everybody to leave happy. We're not striving to win the approval of man. We do, however, hope people leave encouraged, challenged, and blessed by an encounter with God.

Mediocrity is not marvelous. We believe God and his people deserve our very best.

What next?

This Sunday, thank a pastor, worship leader or volunteer for their Kingdom efforts.

May I pray for you?

Lord, you alone are without fault. You alone can attain true excellence. Our efforts fall short; we are perfectly imperfect. But our desire is to give you our best! Amen.

DAY 63: REMEMBERING PHINEAS

"Yet what we suffer now is nothing compared to the glory he will reveal to us later. We know that God works all things together for good for the ones who love God, for those who are called according to his purpose" Romans 8:18, 28 NLT.

I'm not a big fan of looking back. I'd rather look forward. Not for a second do I want to be the old guy who's always talking about the good-ol'-days. But sometimes we have to look at what *was* to fully appreciate what is and what is to come.

I know…sometimes we look back and it stirs a storm of regrets. Sometimes we remember our past with pain and deep sorrow. But who we are today is the result of all that has happened in our lives so far. Our mistakes, our failures and our hurts mold us. Our joys and past successes shape us. Even the sins against us play a role in forming us into the people we are right now.

And here's a greater truth: nothing is beyond God's power to redeem. Nothing is beyond his ability to restore. And therefore, nothing is ever wasted by him. Nothing.

In 2008, my first grandson, Phineas, was born. Due to a premature birth and undeveloped lungs, he only lived an hour. Though I have lost many friends and family members over the years, no death hurt more. Every detail of the first and last time I held Phineas in that hospital room in Portland is forever etched in my mind. The agony and sorrow in my son and daughter-in-law's eyes still brings tears to mine.

It is a memory I sometimes wish I could forget. And if that were all there was—pain and sorrow—those emotions would consume me. But the story doesn't end there.

Somehow, the loss of Phineas has developed in me an even deeper longing for heaven and a hope for what is to come. This world and this life are not all there is. Somehow, the pain of my past has taught me to run to Abba Father and to snuggle close to him when I'm hurting. And somehow, whatever has happened in my life to date reminds me that God is bigger than my circumstances and is always with me no matter what.

What next?
Grow from your past. Press on toward your future. Keep your eyes fixed on the God who works for your benefit.

May I pray for you?
God, the past can be a tool to help us learn or a trap to prevent us from growing. But you never intended for us to get stuck. Through your sacrifice on the cross, we have received restoration. Thank you for freeing us. Help us cast off the chains and move forward. Amen.

DAY 64: DEFINING SUCCESS

"Put God in charge of your work, then what you've planned will take place" Proverbs 16:3 TM.

Most of my life as a child and a young man, I was driven by a need for approval from others. Most of what I did was motivated by an unhealthy performance orientation. If people liked me, gave me kudos, or at least applauded my efforts, I felt good. If not, I found myself in a self-induced funk so twisted it was scary.

Over the years, I've grown. I'm better at living for an audience of One and working for God's glory and not my own. But that little boy who longs too much for an *attaboy* still lurks somewhere in the darkness.

So how is success best defined? Here are my musings....

- Success is measured by obedience. Am I doing what God has asked me to do, and will I do it regardless of the cost?
- Success is determined by the impact of my life for Christ. It's not about me; it's all about him.
- Success is shown in the ripple effect of my actions and words in the lives of others.
- Success is experienced and celebrated when hearts and lives are changed for good.

Not long ago I guest-spoke at a friend's church. At the conclusion of the service, a woman approached me with tears in her eyes. She clutched a copy of my book *Epic Grace: Chronicles of a Recovering Idiot* to her chest as she said, "I bought your book two weeks ago. I didn't even know you were coming to our church! I felt like God put it in my hands. You see, I have a 29-year-old son who is a prodigal, and I'd given up on him. But as I read your words, hope returned to my heart."

By the time she finished telling her story, we were both crying.

The true measure of success in God's kingdom is all about the benefit and blessing you and I bring to others. Whether it's only one other or a million others is up to him.

What next?
What are your plans for success? Have you committed them to the Lord? Do it today!

May I pray for you?
God, we exist on earth for one reason: you. We may scheme, plan, and scramble to reach the top wrung of the proverbial ladder, but without you our attempts are worthless. So we commit our lives and work to you, Lord. May we find success in your economy. Amen.

DAY 65: EMBRACE REJECTION PART 1

"He was oppressed and treated harshly, yet he never said a word. He was led like a lamb to the slaughter. And as a sheep is silent before the shearers, he did not open his mouth" Isaiah 53:7 NLT.

Rejection hurts. It bruises our egos. It messes with our head. We typically wonder, "What's wrong with me?" Or we might become defensive and ask, "What's wrong with them?" Sometimes we even get frustrated with God and cry out, "How could you let this happen to me?"

A while ago I heard someone say, "We have to exercise our willingness to be rejected." My first thought was, *You're kidding, right? How could rejection ever be a good thing?* But after reading Isaiah 53 my perspective changed.

Here's what I'm learning:

- It's better to be humble than proud. The simple truth is, it's healthy to be reminded that I'm not as hot, cool, together, gifted, popular…as I think I am. And let's be honest, sometimes we screw up and are the primary cause of our rebuff. A part of embracing rejection is embracing truth. What might I have done to create this? What can I learn from this?
- It's better to be relational than right. It's better to suck it up and smile than it is to react in anger or

defensiveness. Jesus accepted denunciation and went silently to the cross for the sake of his relationship with us. He was completely right, yet he died.

- It's good to welcome any opportunity to become more like Jesus. Keep in mind, he was despised and denied by some of his closest friends even though he never did anything wrong. Like Jesus, we must learn to please God above all even if our faithful obedience costs us everything. By embracing rejection like Jesus did, we can grow in character and become stronger in our faith.

Please don't misunderstand me. I'm not suggesting we wallow in misery. I'm not telling you to look for occasions to be rejected. And I'm not saying that we should put up with emotional abuse.

What I am saying, however, is that when rejection comes (and it will), view it with a new perspective. Maybe instead of automatically rejecting rejection with disdain or despair, we embrace it as an opportunity to change, to grow, and to become a little bit more like Jesus.

What next?
Read Isaiah 53 and think about other ways we can grow by embracing rejection.

May I pray for you?

Jesus, you are the ultimate expert on rejection. Show us how we can grow in the midst of trials and become more like you. Help us embrace truth and acknowledge our culpability when necessary. Amen.

DAY 66: EMBRACE REJECTION PART 2

"Haven't you read this passage of Scripture: 'The stone the builders rejected has become the cornerstone'" Mark 12:10.

I'll never forget the Sunday years ago when a little old lady cornered me in our tiny church lobby. She made it clear from her body language and facial expression that she was not happy! My talk that morning had pushed her buttons, and she was going to give this young, arrogant pastor a tongue-lashing. I went home that day ready to quit (again).

As a teaching pastor, every Sunday my congregation evaluates me. New attendees compare me to their previous pastor. Regular attenders measure the value of the current talk or series to the last one.

As an author and blogger, other writers scrutinize what I produce, and my copy editor sometimes rips me to shreds. Then, of course, the readers leave their mark by buying or not buying my books or by liking or ignoring my posts.

Rejection is painful, but it has taught me much:

- It teaches me to be humble.
- It helps me learn how to *grow* and not just *go* through disappointment.

- It gives me empathy for others who experience rejection.
- It sometimes brings needed correction to my life.
- It reminds me to forgive as I have been forgiven and to offer grace to those who, like me, don't deserve it.
- It develops the character traits of perseverance and resiliency.
- It reminds me to speak the truth in love even when it's not easy to hear.
- It challenges me to see the big picture and realize it's not about me.
- It causes me to focus on my audience of One.

Do I love rejection? Uh, that would be *no*. But do I see its value better now in my old age than I did when I was young? Yup. Frankly, given the choice, I'd probably choose love and acceptance over the angst of rejection, but it's more of a speed bump in my life now than a dead end. How about you?

What next?

Think of a rejection you've faced. How can you make it a positive event in your life?

May I pray for you?

Jesus, you know better than any of us how difficult rejection can be to live with and overcome. Help us to press through the pain of hurtful words and unjust accusations. Teach us to "count it all joy" when we encounter trials via ignorant (and sometimes cruel) people. Somehow, make us more like you. Amen.

DAY 67: GENERATION GAPS

"Remember the days of old; consider the generations long past. Ask your father and he will tell you, your elders, and they will explain to you" Deuteronomy 32:7.

I had an interesting conversation with a twenty-something not long ago. He told me how hard it is to be a Christian in today's culture. He wasn't really looking for advice, but I gave it to him anyhow. Far be it from me to withhold an unsolicited opinion.

His response didn't really surprise me. I've heard it many times before, "You don't understand my generation. Things are different today than when you were young."

But are things really that different? Here are five things true of every generation:

- Every generation thinks they know better than the generation before them. When I was twenty, I thought my parents were totally out of touch with reality. However, I was cocky in my youthful arrogance, and I failed to realize that there is no substitute for wisdom, and wisdom only comes with age and experience.
- Every generation is significantly influenced by their culture. Go back a thousand years in history and you'll find humans profoundly affected by the

culture around them. Sure, the world was smaller, and the medium for temptations different, but our base human desires have always been the same.

- Every generation wrestles with the same two big questions: Who am I? Why am I here? People are desperate for meaning in their lives. From the beginning of time, we humans have struggled with our identity and purpose.
- Every generation attempts to alter truth to suit their desires and beliefs. We insist on being our own gods. We want to go our own way and do our own thing. Throughout history people have worshiped false gods and false beliefs of their own making.
- Every generation is fascinated by the new, the bigger, and the better. We are always looking for the next thing, the next fashion, or the next trend in technology. But what we think is "hot" now will someday be a forgotten memory.

At the core, every generation deals with the same heart issues, the same human tendencies, and the same proclivity to failure and sin. This has always been true, and it always will be true. People are people.

What next?
If you're old, embrace the new. Adapt. It's okay. You'll be fine. If you're young, accept and appreciate the old. Remember nothing on planet earth lasts forever. Only people do.

May I pray for you?

Lord, only you see the big picture from generation to generation. We view a mere snapshot. Help us depend on you to develop our perspective of life. Amen.

DAY 68: MUCH ADO ABOUT NOTHING

"So we don't look at the troubles we can see now; rather, we fix our gaze on things that cannot be seen. For the things we see now will soon be gone, but the things we cannot see will last forever" 2 Corinthians 4:18.

Admittedly, what matters a great deal to me may not matter at all to you. We're all raised with a set of values that others might not share.

But are there times when we make relatively small issues overly important? Are there things we care about that shouldn't matter so much in the grand scale of life?

- Your computer broke. Bummer. How does that measure up to someone's broken heart?
- Your boss was a jerk yesterday. Sorry. But how does that compare to a person who is facing divorce or the death of a spouse?
- Dang! Your back is killing you. How does your friend with cancer feel?
- You're starving because you skipped lunch today. But do you know how many people will go to bed hungry tonight, and they're literally starving?

When you struggle, do you have a big-picture perspective of life? When you're in the thick of it, can you see past your needs and challenges? Here's a crazy idea: maybe it's not just about you (or me).

I'm convinced the best way to maintain an attitude of gratitude is to remember the needs of others. The secret to "giving thanks in all circumstances" (1 Thess. 5:18) is perspective. "Yeah, my back is bad, but at least I'm not dead yet!" Regardless of your situation, you can always be thankful for something.

When I stop focusing on my problems and see the needs of others around me, it typically motivates me to action, and I find it's "more blessed to give than receive" (Acts 20:35). I develop an eternal perspective and find hope when I remember that nothing, and certainly no problem, lasts forever.

Perspective. It matters. A lot.

What next?
Take a moment today and gain some perspective. Ask the Lord to give you his eyes to see and his ears to hear, then list ten things you're thankful for right now.

May I pray for you?
God, it's easy to believe the universe revolves around us. Give us your perspective, Lord. We want to act in such a way that acknowledges and cares for the needs of others. Turn our hearts toward the things that matter to you. Amen.

DAY 69: THE CHALLENGE OF BEAUTY

"Your beauty should not come from outward adornment, such as elaborate hairstyles and the wearing of gold jewelry or fine clothes. Rather, it should be that of your inner self, the unfading beauty of a gentle and quiet spirit, which is of great worth in God's sight" 1 Peter 3:3-4.

We live in a culture where beauty is relational currency that offers social value. Gorgeous people win the contests, get the attention, and grace the covers of magazines.

If you want to succeed or become famous, you'd better be either really smart or really attractive. Of course, from time to time the not-so-pretty are applauded, but nobody puts their photos on display.

But what if our true value has nothing to do with the image we see in the mirror?

We've all heard the phrase, "Beauty is only skin deep." In a moment of rational thought, we'd all agree that it's important to be beautiful on the inside, not just the outside. More often than not, however, we aspire to be tall, skinny, wrinkle and blemish-free, and with hair to die for.

But what if we saw others and ourselves from a different perspective?

I am not advocating for ugliness. I'm not saying that physical beauty is meaningless. I am, however, challenging a belief system that elevates physical beauty above what really matters.

Eventually, beauty fades. Age and gravity win. You can nip and tuck all you want, but sooner or later the person staring back at you from the bathroom mirror will be old and far from stunning. And if your value comes only from an outward beauty, then that relational currency will leave you bankrupt and feeling pretty miserable in the end.

However, if you are a man or woman who has loved God and loved people—that beauty lasts forever. If you are a person who lives and walks in grace—that makes you stunning until your last breath.

Go ahead, be beautiful (it's okay), but most of all, be beautiful where it *really* counts.

What next?
Today, be beautiful by loving God and people. Build relational currency with eternal value.

May I pray for you?
God, may we reflect our inner beauty through our interactions with people today. Amen.

DAY 70: THE CHURCH IS IRRELEVANT!

"The Spirit of the Lord is on me. He has anointed me to tell the good news to poor people. He has sent me to announce freedom for prisoners. He has sent me so that the blind will see again. He wants me to free those who are beaten down" Luke 4:18 NIRV.

I've been in the Church almost my entire life. For the past 57 years (except for about a year or so when I wandered), I've attended church gatherings faithfully at numerous denominations, including the non-denominational church I pastor now.

You might think my varied background in the Church would make me confused. However, my experience has given me a great deal of clarity: I know the Church is not a building. It's not an hour on Sunday. It's bigger than our pet peeves, our pet doctrines, and our pet organizational structures. And it's far from perfect.

I also know the Church is irrelevant! Unless...

- Unless she is more of an *organism* than an *organization*.
- Unless she provides a place for community, celebration expressed through vibrant worship, public baptisms, Holy Communion, and authentic and relevant teaching.

- Unless she motivates and engages her members to live otherly-focused.
- Unless she becomes a safe place for people to discover God's grace and to develop along their journey of faith.
- Unless she engages all involved to realize and utilize their spiritual gifts.
- Unless she pools her human and financial resources to do more together than any one individual can do alone.
- Unless she provides a place for the demonstration of the glory and power of God to transform broken lives and to heal broken bodies.

We simply can't play church. We can't do church. We must *be* the Church, which means we must act just like Jesus.

What next?

Take risks. Go to gatherings (wherever they may be) with a desperate and expectant heart. Hold on to important values and practices while being willing to venture into the unknown. Yield to and live filled by the Holy Spirit.

May I pray for you?

God, we are the Church. You have called us beyond buildings and denominations to spread your Word throughout the nations. Our prayer is that as Christians, we would set aside irrelevancies and focus together on what matters most: loving you and loving people. Amen.

DAY 71: UNMET EXPECTATIONS

"If you've gotten anything at all out of following Christ... then do me a favor: Agree with each other, love each other, be deep-spirited friends. Don't push your way to the front; don't sweet-talk your way to the top. Put yourself aside, and help others get ahead. Don't be obsessed with getting your own advantage..." Philippians 2:1-4 TM.

We all live with expectations. We expect certain things from our family, our friends, our employer, our church, the government, and yup—from God himself. And just about everyone who's anyone of significance in your life has expectations of you.

Some are spoken. Some are implied. Some are reasonable. Some are not. But all of us live in a world with expectations. When our expectations are met, we tend to be happy. When they are forgotten, ignored, or denied...well...let's just say that things can get pretty ugly.

So what do you do? How should we handle unmet expectations? Here are a few thoughts:

- Step back and try to see the bigger picture. Believe it or not, it's not all about you or me. Maybe the other person is wrestling with a bigger issue than our immediate need or desire.
- Believe the best rather than assume the worst. Until

proven wrong, give people the benefit of the doubt.

- Adjust your expectations to better match your performance. Have you noticed that you hold others to a higher standard than you live by? It's not fair or wise to expect more from someone else than we expect from ourselves.

- Decide to walk in mercy and grace. Mercy is being spared from the grief we deserve; grace is getting the favor we don't. When I stop to think about how many times I haven't met God's expectations and yet how often I have received his mercy and grace—it humbles me. I can give some of that unmerited goodness to others.

Having expectations isn't wrong. It's normal. But how we handle unmet expectations is important.

What next?
Think about the last conflict you had with someone. Was an unmet expectation at the heart of it? What are you willing to do for the sake of peace?

May I pray for you?
God, help us love people and put each other's needs before our own. When we feel let down because of unmet expectations, remind us to walk in mercy and grace. Examine our hearts and show us how to live in peace. Amen.

DAY 72: FORTUNE COOKIES

"'My thoughts are nothing like your thoughts,' says the LORD. 'And my ways are far beyond anything you could imagine'" Isaiah 55:8 NLT.

At the end of our meal at the local Mongolian BBQ, the waitress brought my wife and I fortune cookies with our bill. As cookies go, they aren't that great, but I eat them nonetheless. And this time, the message inside got me wondering: can God speak through a fortune cookie?

My Mongolian BBQ fortune that night said, "Your experiences this week will all make good sense within the year."

Hmm…. I'd had some amazingly good and terribly bad experiences that very week, and my mind was reeling from a bunch of things that didn't make any sense. What did I do wrong? What could I have done better? Why is God so good to me even when I don't deserve it?

I know it sounds mystical to suggest that God spoke to me through a cookie, but if God is God, and he is sovereign and powerful, can't he use anything he chooses to get our attention?

Remember the story of Balaam and his donkey in Numbers 22? God used an animal to speak to a guy who was way off course. Weird? Yup. Mystical? Oh yeah. Real? Absolutely.

Now, I'm *not* suggesting that donkey-talk or cookie-talk is normal. I'm certainly not encouraging you to look for God's voice or direction in a can of alphabet soup or in your next crossword puzzle. That being said, I do want to remind you that God is enigmatic. In fact, it seems he sometimes delights in offending our sensibleness with his awe-inspiring mysteriousness. Please don't box God into your little rational and explainable world. He's bigger than you think. His ways are not our ways, and sometimes he will absolutely surprise you.

So get in the Word. Get godly counsel. Get on your knees. When something unusual and unexpected happens, pray and cry out, "God are you trying to get my attention? Is there something here I need to see or know?"

What next?

Have you ever questioned an unusual encounter with God? What became of the situation? Did hindsight offer clarity?

May I pray for you?

God, help us discern your voice, whether or not it comes from unexpected places. Amen.

DAY 73: GOD BLESS AMERICA?

"But our citizenship is in heaven. And we eagerly await a Savior from there, the Lord Jesus Christ..." Philippians 3:20.

Does God bless a nation? Does he want to sanctify us as a country? If we collectively get our moral and spiritual act together, can we expect better times?

What would that look like?

- Does it mean God will bless us financially if as a society we return to his Word and his ways?
- Does it mean he will give us peace and protection from our enemies if we acknowledge him as Americans?
- Does it mean we can expect to have life, liberty, and justice for all if we do a better job of turning our nation back to Christ?

Some will declare, "Our country was founded on biblical principles by godly men who embraced the truths of Scripture. We have been 'one nation under God' from the beginning." Really? Have you read the history books?

Were we one nation under God when we defeated and mistreated the indigenous people of this land? Were we one nation under God when we trafficked in slavery and abused Africans for our own benefit? Has God blessed

America because we've always been so good, so right, and so holy? Or it is possible that God blessed his people (Christ-followers), and thus a nation benefitted?

When you say, "God bless America!" and you mean, "God, bless your people so that they can be a blessing to others," I'm all for it! But if you want God to bless a political party or a political system or even a place on the map, then you won't get an *amen* from me.

I pray for our country, but not with a view to some faceless group called Americans. I pray for the Church. I pray that we who call on the Lord will influence our country for him. God wants his people to be a blessing to this nation and to the whole world.

What next?
What is your hope for our country? Today, focus on loving its people.

May I pray for you?
God, bless your people (wherever they may be found) to bless the land they live in (wherever that may be). May our lives honor you. Amen.

DAY 74: SPIRITUAL ADD

"Brothers and sisters, I do not consider myself yet to have taken hold of it. But one thing I do: Forgetting what is behind and straining toward what is ahead, I press on toward the goal to win the prize for which God has called me heavenward in Christ Jesus" Philippians 3:13-14.

Being easily distracted is something I've wrestled with for years. As a child, my instructors sat me in the front row or right next to the teacher's desk. I was infamous for going about ten directions at once (or trying to). Back then ADD and ADHD weren't on anyone's radar, but I'm sure I suffered from one of them.

Recently, I've noticed another type of ADD in the Church. Christ-followers are finding it harder and harder to stay focused on what truly matters.

For example, we get sidetracked by whether it's okay for Christians to drink (in moderation) or have a tattoo, while every day over 100,000 babies are aborted worldwide. We fight over our theological pet peeves, like whether the gifts of the Spirit are relevant for today or not, while millions of children go to sleep every night in hunger. Do we really want to fight each other over the non-essential, minor things of life, or fight together for justice and the poor?

What's the solution? Let me give you a few things you can do to avoid spiritual ADD:

- Stay close to the Teacher. Listen to him. Watch him. Get to know what Jesus thinks and how he feels. If you are a disciple of Jesus, you must stay close to him to become more like him.
- Stay faithful to the values of the Kingdom. His ways are better than our ways. His plan is better than our plan. When we love and value what he loves and values (like people), we will live like he lived.
- Stay put and grow where God planted you. Guess what? In my experience, we grow best through hardship and struggle. Like an evergreen on the Washington coast, we are made stronger as we're buffeted by the winds and rain. The storms of life are often a source of life.

Spiritual ADD is a struggle for a lot of us. We live in a world filled with distractions. So lean on Jesus for the help you need, and watch what God can do.

What next?
What distracts you? Does it have eternal importance? Get refocused today.

May I pray for you?

Lord, we want to focus on what matters. Show us what is important to you, and give us the ability to stay the course even as life threatens to derail us. Amen.

DAY 75: VALIDATION

"See what great love the Father has lavished on us, that we should be called children of God! And that is what we are!" 1 John 3:1.

Maybe you've been to an office building or a shopping venue where they charged you to park. Isn't it nice, however, when you get to hand the attendant a get-out-of-jail-free parking stub because somebody validated you?

We treasure validation in our personal relationships. When someone says, "I really appreciate you," we walk away from that encounter feeling pretty good. When others recognize our achievements, it strokes our ego and affirms our sense of worth.

For way too much of my life I've lived with a performance mentality. My belief system said, "If I perform well, succeed, and look good, then others will love me." That created an unholy need for validation birthed out of a false belief that my performance determines my worth.

Validation in and of itself is not evil. In fact, building each other up through encouragement is good. The Word says in Ephesians 4:29, "Do not let any unwholesome talk come out of your mouths, but only what is helpful for building others up according to their needs, that it may benefit those who listen." Blessing someone through the power of our words is righteous.

But when does validation become a problem? Here's the answer: when the need for validation becomes the driving force in our lives. It's okay until it becomes what we live for.

Do you strive for the applause of others because without it you wither? Do you frequently fish for compliments because without them you become discouraged or depressed? Do your insecurities cause you to regard what people think more than what God thinks? If so, seeking validation is a problem.

The truth is, my accomplishments don't reflect my eternal worth. My value to God is based on the fact he created me and unconditionally loves me, because it is his nature to love. It all starts and ends with him.

So relax. Be at peace. Rest in God's validation. Stop requiring the approval of men, because you already have the approval of God through Christ.

What next?
Next time you need an attaboy or attagirl in order to feel good—remember your worth in Jesus. His love for you cannot be earned through any achievement or lost through any failure.

May I pray for you?

God, your love for us stretches far beyond what our eyes can see. Thank you for adopting us into your family and calling us sons and daughters. May we always seek validation in you. Amen.

DAY 76: CRYING OUT

"The eyes of the Lord are on those who do what is right and good. His ears are open to their cry" Psalm 34:15 NLV.

Early one morning, my grandson Elijah startled me awake with a loud cry. (Gotta love baby monitors!) His parents had stolen away for an overnighter and left their kids in our loving care. I don't know if Elijah's dreams had disturbed him, or if he'd roused only to find himself in an unfamiliar and dark place, but whatever the reason, he woke up afraid and crying. Of course, both Grandma and Grandpa rushed to his side to comfort him.

As I tried to go back to sleep, I thought, *Who do we cry to when we find ourselves in a dark, scary, and unfamiliar place?* The tragic truth is, sometimes we self-medicate when terrified. Sometimes we try to cover our fear with "things" that only complicate our situation rather than alleviate it. And sadly, sometimes in our scariest moments, we cry out for the wrong comforter.

In the past, during unsettling events, how have you responded to fear and the unknown?

Your child was diagnosed with cancer, and you turned to alcohol to numb your senses. You lost your job, and you distracted yourself from reality with a whirlwind shopping spree. Your marriage began to fail, and you sought solace in someone else's arms.

Here's a better way: the best thing we can do is cry out to the one who has the power to calm and console our anxious hearts. And, as any dad (or granddad) would, he will come rushing to our side!

What next?

Are you facing an overwhelming situation—a sick child, a lost job, a failing marriage, an insurmountable task, or a hopeless future? Get on your knees and cry out to the Lord. There is no dark corner his light can't reach. There is no life he can't redeem.

May I pray for you?

God, we have all experienced fear. Life is full of unknowns and threatening situations. Be our light in the darkness. Be our hope and salvation. Answer us when we cry out to you, and comfort us when we're scared. Amen.

DAY 77: HABITS

"This has been my practice: I obey your precepts" Psalm 119:56.

Habits are good (at least the good ones are good). We all have them. We all follow a routine of some sort and complete many tasks with predictable regularity.

- You probably order your coffee the same way every time.
- You prefer one side of the bed over another.
- You like your steak cooked a certain way.
- Many of us start to brush our teeth on the same side without even thinking about it.
- Some practice a daily routine of prayer, Bible reading, and journaling.

We're human, and we homo sapiens like our routines. They offer us a measure of comfort. They provide patterns in our lives that assist us in our daily duties. In fact, without habits we would go crazy trying to remember the millions of little things we do without a thought.

On the last day of a recent working vacation it struck me, *Wow. I haven't written much, prayed much, or exercised at all.* All of my normal activities were disrupted by a different environment and an unusual schedule.

You might say, "A break in routine is good for the soul." And I would agree. However, some habits are always important. For instance, my dentist would insist that brushing my teeth at least twice a day is a good idea, even on vacation. I'm pretty sure God would say it's never wise to stop healthy spiritual habits. In fact, spiritual disciplines are more important than physical ones.

So where am I going with this? What have I learned? Teeth are temporary; my soul is not. I need to establish good spiritual practices no matter what and no matter where. If I've discovered anything about myself it's this simple reality: I leak (and so do you). Without routine spiritual habits, I eventually start to drift and wither. I've also learned that I find a way to accomplish what's important to me.

How about you?

What next?
If you've noticed a lag in your spiritual disciplines, make a commitment to start fresh today.

May I pray for you?
God, we need you. You are food and drink for our souls. Without you our spirits starve. Help us establish a routine of ingesting your Word and consuming your presence. Remind us how important daily time with you is so that we can grow in spiritual health. Amen.

DAY 78: HOW TO DEAL
WITH DISTRACTIONS

"My eyes are ever on the Lord, for only he will release my feet from the snare" Psalm 25:15.

A while back I joined a close pastor friend for a cup of coffee. Often, God speaks into my life through this guy, and this time was no exception.

I shared with him a few minor financial and relational struggles. As I sipped my Americano, he looked me in the eye and said, "Those things are just foxes meant to distract you. Stay focused on Jesus, Kurt."

Years ago, I visited a friend in Scotland. He told me a story about one pesky little fox who often stole into his chicken coop and ran off with his best egg-layers. He'd sit in his attic for hours, window open and rifle in hand, hoping to nab the wily critter.

With the expectation of a victorious story, I asked him, "Well, did you ever get him?" "Blimey, no!" he said, "I just wasted a lot of time sitting in my attic like a silly twit."

That's what foxes do; they keep you worried about the chickens and wasting way too much time in the process. So how should we deal with a fox? Here are some things to consider:

- What might be lost or negatively affected by this fox? If it's something important, kill the dang fox. If it's not truly critical, you might be better off ignoring it.
- Has this fox become so consuming in your life that you forget what truly matters? Again, you might have to destroy the fox to get free from it, but maybe it's just a ploy of the enemy to rob you of your peace in Christ.
- Is the fox rabid? For example, pornography is not a fox, and neither is a divisive person (that person is a wolf). Don't excuse a major issue by calling it a fox. See the problem for what it is and deal with it accordingly.
- Is this fox the *source* of your difficulty or a *symptom* of something deeper? The best way to take care of symptomatic problems is to treat the root issue.

Ask Jesus to show you whether or not a fox is worthy of your attention. He will. Be wise and stay aware. Our enemy doesn't always send grizzlies after us, but rather annoying little foxes meant to draw our eyes off Jesus.

What next?
Think about the foxes in your life, and decide whether it's best to ignore or kill them.

May I pray for you?

Lord, we are prone to distractions. Keep our eyes on you, and release us from the snares we stumble into. Help us discern foxes from grizzlies. Amen.

DAY 79: WHY TRUST MATTERS

"Do all that you can to live in peace with everyone"
Romans 12:18 NLT.

Trust is at the core of every healthy relationship. When you trust someone, your mind is at peace, and simply the thought of that person brings you joy. When it is broken, however, there is an unsettling pain at even the mention of the offender's name.

Trust provides an environment of confidence in a relationship. It fosters an openness that allows us to speak the truth in love. But without trust, it's hard to believe the best about another person, let alone take the risk of being honest with them.

When we trust, our fears and worries are greatly reduced (if not eliminated). When we don't, we can easily become consumed by an overwhelming need to control and micromanage.

Trust matters. So what happens when trust is broken? Is it possible to rebuild and restore what has been lost? Yes, but it takes time and lots of hard work.

- The first step toward healing is complete and utter transparency. The offender must own his or her sin without any "yeah-buts." It's never okay to rationalize or justify sin. Ever. Sure, others probably failed as well, but the only way to rebuild trust is to take full responsibility for your actions. Period.

- The next step involves a willingness to accept the consequences. The wrongdoer can and should be forgiven, but mercy and grace don't always eliminate "reaping what is sown." When we are willing to accept the repercussions of our actions, it builds trust because it demonstrates humility.
- The final step is the hardest one because it's not something we humans typically enjoy: waiting. The rebuilding of trust is a process and sometimes a slow one.

Picture trust as a bridge that has been damaged or destroyed. The resulting gap is great and the challenges ahead are difficult, but not insurmountable. There are no shortcuts, however. It simply takes time. Time to heal. Time to earn again the trust that was lost. Time to rebuild the bridge.

Regaining trust involves believing again in a way that restores faith and hope in the offender. How could that not be worth the time and effort?

What next?
Have you or a loved one broken trust? Do your part to restore what was lost, and pray the other person does too. Then watch and see what God can do!

May I pray for you?

God, you are always faithful. People make mistakes, but you never fail. We're grateful that we can trust you in all things. Help us offer grace and forgiveness to those who wrong us and to humbly apologize when we are the offenders. Amen.

DAY 80: I SWEAR!

"Don't use foul or abusive language. Let everything you say be good and helpful, so that your words will be an encouragement to those who hear them" Ephesians 4:29 NLT.

About ten years ago, I attended a conference where a nationally known pastor spoke. He was good, passionate, engaging, and he swore. Some in the crowd smiled. Others gasped. "Did he just say what I think he said?" Yup.

I remember thinking, "Cool. If he can do it, so can I!" Like William Wallace in *Braveheart*, my soul cried, "Freedom!" I didn't use crass or crude language, but I did begin to cross the line of propriety.

Fast forward to a conversation with my wife on a road trip. She said, in her gentle way, "Honey, I don't understand why you like to use those words, and it concerns me."

For the next couple of hours on I-90, I did a lot of reflecting. I've always resisted being put on a super-saint religious pedestal, and I saw my language as a means to being a real pastor in a real world.

Then God had the audacity to interrupt my rationalizations. "This is a heart issue," he whispered. That's not what I expected or wanted to hear.

There was no denying the fact that the overwhelming majority of time I used bad language was because of something bad in my heart.

For the record, here's where I've landed: I can be relevant without being rude. I can be real without being foul. And I can be holy without being hypocritical.

Truth is, I simply want to be more like Jesus, and I find it hard to imagine him saying anything unwholesome or unholy.

What next?

Ask yourself what's in your heart when you color the air with your words. Is everything you say "good and helpful…and an encouragement to those who hear" you? If not, maybe it's time to reevaluate the way you speak.

May I pray for you?

God, we are surrounded by a culture that embraces crude and vulgar language. Sometimes we get sucked in as well. Help us assess our hearts before we speak and to honor you with our words. Our desire is to become more like you. Amen.

DAY 81: THE FAST AND THE FURIOUS!

"Whoever loses his life for my sake will find it" Matthew 10:39.

One of the great paradoxes of Scripture is that we find life when we willingly lose it by giving it to God. This doesn't mean that we earn our salvation or God's favor, but it does mean that we experience his favor more fully when we earnestly seek him and faithfully obey him.

I hate to fast; it makes me furious! (I love food and food loves me!) But what makes me even more furious is the brokenness I see all around me in this city and in our world.

Fasting is one of the most feared and misunderstood practices in the Bible. It's feared because we all love food, and it's often misunderstood because we think only fanatics fast. It flies in the face of our culture that is all about satisfying our needs and desires with very little (if any) concern for denial or self-sacrifice.

Let me define what fasting is and isn't:

- Fasting is the spiritual discipline of willingly sacrificing something we value. Fasting is *not* a means to manipulate God through a spiritual hunger strike.

- The word "fast" in both the Hebrew (tsom) and Greek (nesteia) refers to the practice of self-denial. The key concept is abstinence for a spiritual purpose. Fasting is *not* self-sacrifice used to placate the anger of God. He's not mad at you; he's mad about you!
- In the Old Testament, sometimes people fasted when they were brokenhearted (such as David and his men in 2 Sam. 11). Fasting is *not* penance for sin. Our debt is paid in full!
- In the New Testament, there are examples of leaders and the church fasting when in need of divine guidance or facing a new ministry challenge (Acts 13 & 14). Fasting is *not* a religious ritual done to impress others (Jesus addressed this in Matt. 6:16-18).

I like to describe fasting as prayer on steroids because it enhances the intensity of your heart-cry to God. It's almost always an act of desperation for the intervention and manifestation of God in your midst.

Simply put: fasting is about God and for God. And it's important to understand that fasting is not so much about us getting his attention as it is about him getting ours. (Go back and read that last sentence again.)

What next?
This week, take a day to fast and pray.

May I pray for you?

God, we tend to avoid discomfort. But sometimes we need to move toward it for a purpose. Nudge us in the right direction, and turn our hearts toward you in obedience. Amen.

DAY 82: LIFE IS HARD

"Be joyful in hope, patient in affliction, faithful in prayer" Romans 12:12.

Sometimes life is hard, and I don't mean just "having a bad hair day" hard. I mean the kind of hard that knocks you down and then kicks you in the teeth without any mercy.

Sure, there are plenty of high points in life too. I've climbed mountains, trekked the Himalayas, finished two marathons, sailed the Caribbean where pirates once roamed, and walked city streets from Hollywood to Hong Kong. All of these exciting experiences are treasured memories, but I've discovered that most of life's lessons are not taught in the high moments of adventure. Most of what I've learned has come from the dark valleys of defeat and despair.

The word perseverance is not one of my favorite words. To persevere is to keep going no matter what. It means to carry on and continue regardless of the hardship.

Endure. Stick to it. Hang in there. Persevere. I'd really rather not, thank you very much. I'd rather quit. I'd rather complain like a cranky baby with a dirty diaper. I'd rather blame somebody—anybody else. But God says enduring hardship and suffering is admirable.

There are things I don't understand. Frankly, there are lots of things I don't have any answers to. I struggle from time to time with canned Christian clichés about "a greater purpose." I know God can bring good out of any evil, but when you are in the middle of the evil, the darkness can seem overwhelming.

But, here's what I do know; it is the simple truth I learned from a children's song years ago: *Jesus loves me....*

That's about it. That is all I know for sure and it is enough for me.

What next?
Where are you hurting right now? Take that pain to the Lord. He loves you more than his own life.

May I pray for you?
Jesus, you are the expert on perseverance through suffering. You've endured unimaginable pain and hardship for our sake, and you understand our distress when life feels unbearable. Comfort us, guide us, and give us hope in all circumstances. Amen.

DAY 83: WASTED FOR JESUS

"I assure you, wherever the Good News is preached throughout the world, this woman's deed will be talked about in her memory" Mark 14:9 NLT.

Relax, this is not about getting drunk or high. It's about expensive perfume that was "wasted" on Jesus when it could have been sold for a lot of money. However, what the disciples saw as extravagant squander, Jesus viewed as extraordinary adoration.

The scene: Jesus and the disciples are in the town of Bethany, a short distance from Jerusalem. According to Mark's gospel (Mark 14:1-9), Simon the leper hosts a dinner at his home with Jesus as the honored guest.

Custom dictated that the host would anoint Jesus's head with a drop of nard, a pure and expensive perfume. But a woman, Mary, enters the room with an alabaster flask, and she pours *all* the perfume (worth about a year's wages) over Jesus's head and feet. She then dries his feet with her hair.

In that culture, women didn't touch a male to whom they weren't related, and certainly not a Rabbi, so there is tension in the room as Mary literally lets her hair down and caresses her Lord. Shocked by her lack of discretion, the disciples "scolded her harshly."

Jesus comes to Mary's rescue and tells the guys, "leave her alone . . . why berate her for doing such a good thing to me?" He understood what they did not: love is sometimes extravagant and reckless. The disciples saw Mary's act as a misuse of resources; Jesus saw it as a timeless and selfless act of adoration. So what can we learn from Mary?

- An act of adoration will cost you, others will often misunderstand it, but it will always be accepted and valued by Jesus.
- True adoration expressed to Jesus will stand the test of time and God will never forget it. Everything we do for the Kingdom of God has eternal value.
- If you have to be told to do it, then it's *not* an act of adoration. True adoration flows from a humbled heart. It is the response of someone amazed by God's love.

Just like Mary of Bethany, we all have access to Jesus. She demonstrated selfless love and passionate adoration not because she *had* to, but because she *wanted* to.

What next?
What will you do for God as an expression of your love? It might not be practical, logical or reasonable. It may be a sacrifice. But whatever you give in love is precious in his sight.

May I pray for you?

God, you love us without restriction! We want to show you adoration like Mary did. Remove our self-imposed limitations so that we can worship you fully. Amen.

DAY 84: A DESPERATE LONGING

"As the deer pants for streams of water, so my soul pants for you, my God" Psalm 42:1.

If God showed up like a cosmic genie and offered you anything you wanted, what would you request? A hundred billion dollars? A husband or wife? A child? Physical healing? World peace? Maybe you'd ask for unlimited wishes (that would be a good one).

Your first thought is likely what consumes your heart and mind. Our wishes reveal our wants, dreams and desires. Most people don't need to be asked twice about what they crave most. It's right there, at the very top of our mental gotta-have-it list.

As I lay in bed the other night thinking (it's what I do when I can't sleep), I heard the Lord whisper to my heart, "What one thing do you long for above everything else?" Without a moment's hesitation, I said out loud, "Lord, I just long for more of you."

I suppose if I was seriously sick, I would have asked God for healing. If bankrupt, I probably would have asked for financial blessing. But because I hunger for more of him, my answer came easy. My soul aches in a way that cannot be quenched by anything else but the Lord.

Why do we worry and fret over things that truly are of such little consequence? Why do we struggle and strive for things we don't really need?

Sometimes our bodies are damaged. Sometimes our hearts break. Sometimes nothing remains in our wallets. I understand the realities of this world. But often our earthly desires are just that—earthly, temporal, and passing. Compared to everything else in your life, Abba alone is eternal.

Wishes are not always evil. Dreams are not always unholy. I sincerely believe that God loves to bless his kids. That being said, only one desire should come before all others: a desire and longing for him.

What next?
Imagine with me the impact of a life fully consumed by a radical desire for more Jesus. Take one scenario from your thoughts and live it out today.

May I pray for you?
God, it's so easy for us to become consumed by our earthly aspirations. The world tells us that happiness and fulfillment come from money, prestige, health, and physical pleasure. But we know only in you will our yearnings be satisfied. Keep our hearts hungering for you, Lord, and remind us to seek you when we're tempted by worldly pursuits. Amen.

DAY 85: HOW TO HAVE AN AFFAIR

"'For this reason a man will leave his father and mother and be united to his wife, and the two will become one flesh'…. Therefore what God has joined together, let no one separate" Matthew 19:5-6.

Let's take a brief look at the anatomy of an affair and how to have one (if you want to ruin everything):

- Ignore all reasonable and wise boundaries with the opposite sex. Go out for coffee, or better yet for lunch or dinner.
- Flirt because it's fun. Use lots of flattery as well.
- If you're a woman, show as much skin as you can get away with.
- Guys, make sure you compliment the gal on how good she looks, smells, or smiles.
- When the accidental physical contact happens, take advantage of it, and make sure it's mutual.
- Share your deepest fears, thoughts, or feelings with the opposite sex.
- Don't forget to let your mind go crazy. Imagine being with someone else…someone who is fun and exciting.
- Last of all, and this is critical, compare your new friend's amazing strengths and qualities to your spouse's weaknesses.

If you religiously follow the above suggestions, I guarantee you will "succeed" at having an affair in no time. Of course, it might cost your marriage, a lot of money, your peace, many holidays and priceless moments with your kids, possibly your faith, and the respect and admiration of your family, co-workers, and friends. Be sure to count the cost.

Crazy? Yup. There's a better way to live.

Invest in your marriage with diligence. Stay true to your wedding vows. Delight in the spouse of your youth. Get help early when problems arise. Remember that love is a choice more than an emotion.

And if by chance you've failed along the way, run to God's mercy and grace. It's never too late to be forgiven and restored.

What next?
If you're married, take stock of your relationship. Initiate steps to strengthen the bond between you and your spouse today.

May I pray for you?
God, marriage is hard! Help us navigate the ups and downs, and adhere to the vows we made. Teach us to love unconditionally regardless of fleeting emotions. Protect our marriages from temptation and ruin. Amen.

DAY 86: WINNERS AND LOSERS

"If I must boast, I will boast of the things that show my weakness" 2 Corinthians 11:30.

We live in a world that measures a person's worth by the caliber of their performance. From the time we enter school as little children, we are evaluated, judged, and assessed by how well we do in comparison to others.

The difference between first place and no place might be a matter of a few points or milliseconds, but the losers are soon forgotten and the winners go on to further glory (and mega-bucks).

I'm not suggesting that everyone who competes should get gold. But is it right to assign greater value to others simply because they perform better?

Be the best you can be. Go for the prize. Strive for excellence. Absolutely. But is it possible that we have forgotten to treat everyone with the love, respect, and admiration due to *all* as precious individuals created in the image of God? Is it possible that we have become so enamored with the best that we have rejected people whom God accepts?

Jesus talked about caring for the "least of these" (Matthew 25). The Apostle Paul said, "Honor one another above yourselves" (Romans 12). Many of the men and women God chose to use in the Scriptures (from Moses and Rahab to Peter and Paul) were flawed, imperfect, and damaged goods.

It seems to me the standard in Scripture is extremely countercultural. We are admonished to love the unlovely, to value the seemingly insignificant, and to cherish others based on who they are, not just what they do.

Truth is, I'm a loser. No matter how well I do something, there's always going to be someone who can do it better. But when it's all said and done, it's not about me; it's all about God.

Always remember this: God delights in revealing his grace and glory through the broken, the weak, the least of the least, and through losers (like you and me).

What next?

Do you define winning and losing based on God's criteria or the world's? Maybe it's time to reassess your value, and the value of others, according to the Word.

May I pray for you?

Jesus, you told us that the first will be last and the last will be first. The winners will be losers and the losers will be winners. Recalibrate our views of success and excellence so that they match your values. May we strive to win in the areas that please you. Amen.

DAY 87: EXPIRATION DATE

"For that is what God is like. He is our God forever and ever, and he will guide us until we die" Psalm 48:14 NLT.

Death. The word sounds dark and foreboding, and it's not something we like to think about. I've lost fathers, grandparents, aunts, uncles, good friends and a grandson. It struck me recently that the longer I live, the more death I will experience. (Not a happy thought, by the way.) Death is hard to deal with.

Reality is we're all dying. None of us will avoid our last breath in these earth-suits. Some die tragically. Some die unexpectedly. Some die young, and some die very, very old. But all die. Last time I checked, the mortality rate was still at 100%.

How should we live with the reality of our mortality? Let me make a few suggestions:

- Live to make every moment count. Live fully and on purpose so that today doesn't become a regret tomorrow. Pastor and author, Greg Boyd, tweeted this comment on March 18, 2012, "Each and every moment is utterly unprecedented, entirely unrepeatable, exploding with novelty and dancing in God." His point and mine: live today (right now) with intention and passion.

- Live in relational health with others. The Bible is full of admonition to do the best you can to have wholesome and holy relationships with the people in your world. Life is too short to let hatred, anger, pride and bitterness consume you.
- Live without fear. We humans look at life in a linear way with our focus on a beginning and an end. We celebrate our birthdays and mourn the day of death. God, however, knows that we were created as eternal beings, and his plan is for us to live forever with him. You see, this life is just a blip on the radar screen, but even death cannot rob us of our future glory in God. (Check out 2 Cor. 4:18.) The best is yet to come!

I mourn the personal loss of those who have gone on before me. I ache over our temporary separation. I miss them all. But even in the midst of my darkest struggle and deepest agony, I must remember this life is not all there is. In the meantime, I'm going to live with purpose and hope rather than in futility and fear.

What next?
Think about how you might live differently today if you knew it was your last day on planet earth.

May I pray for you?
God, you know the number of our days. Show us how to use them to glorify you. Help us live with intention and purpose, and without fear. Amen.

DAY 88: HURTING FRIENDS

"Above all, love each other deeply, because love covers a multitude of sins" 1 Peter 4:8.

It was unintentional and without evil motivation or wicked design. I didn't mastermind a plan to damage this person or our relationship. In fact, I acted thinking it was best for all concerned, but it wasn't.

Ever been there? You try to avoid stepping in a pile of poo only to find yourself knee deep in it. You honestly expected something good, or at least not something awful, but the result was messed up nonetheless.

When this happens to me, I usually become self-absorbed with regret and disappointment. I can't sleep. I *can* eat (way too much comfort food). And I keep replaying what happened over and over in my brain-damaged noggin as if somehow reliving the experience will change something.

Note to self: it doesn't.

So what should we do in the face of our brokenness and humanity? Here are some things to consider:

- Get real. There was only one person who ever walked on planet earth without sin, and it's not you or me. I find great comfort in the words of Psalm 103:14

(NLT), "God knows how weak we are; he remembers we are only dust." God gets us. He knows better than we do the weakness of our flesh.

- Get forgiven. The best and only real antidote to failure is forgiveness. We must ask God to forgive us. We must ask the offended to forgive us. And in the end, we must forgive ourselves. Forgiveness frees us from the ugly cycle of regret, self-anger, and despair.
- Get better. I wish I mastered every lesson without mistakes, but I seem to learn the hard way. What matters most, however, is growing. So let your failures teach and mold you into a better man or woman of God.

Love covers. It covers our idiocy. It covers our mistakes. It covers our sins. Mine and yours. I've decided to live loved when I fail and love others deeply when they fail me.

What next?
Have you hurt someone lately? Get real, get forgiven, get better and live loved!

May I pray for you?
God, sometimes we're idiots. We hurt those we love. We make mistakes. We sin. Forgive us, Lord. Thank you for modeling love so that by your example we can offer it to others. Help us grow through our experiences and become the people you intend us to be. Amen.

DAY 89: WILL WORK FOR LOVE

"So Jacob worked seven years for Rachel. But it only seemed like a few days, he loved her so much" Genesis 29:20 TM.

When I was sixteen years old, I gave my heart to my wife and she's held it close ever since. The years haven't always been easy (I am, after all, a recovering idiot), but I'd still choose her, and she'd still choose me. I am a blessed man indeed!

Maintaining love takes work, however. Here are four things I've learned along the way:

- It ain't always easy. Romance is but a recurring season (it comes and goes), and sometimes we're not even sure we *like* each other let alone *love* each other. You'd think after several decades together my wife and I wouldn't say stupid stuff or do hurtful things to each other. We do. You'd think by now we'd be communication experts. We're not. You'd think we'd figure out how to live selflessly. We haven't. Love ain't easy. Never has been. Probably never will be.
- It will cost you to truly love. Anything and everything of value costs us time, energy, and money. To love your spouse means sometimes you will sacrifice your agenda and schedule to satisfy theirs. It means sometimes you will serve them even when you're

dead-dog tired. It means sometimes you will invest your hard-earned cash to bless them rather than spend it (or waste it) on what you want. Sacrifice. Service. Investment. Yup…love will cost you.

- It takes a "sticky" attitude to survive. When it's more convenient to bail out rather than work through it, you'll take the path of least resistance unless you're committed to sticking it out over the long haul. Stick-to-it-tiveness is missing in many marriages today. However, love that is sticky is love that will last.
- It's always worth it. I can't promise you a pony or a prize for hanging in there, but I can promise you joy. Joy is the result of spending your life with someone who is broken (like you) and weathering the storms with faith in a God who is bigger and better than your spouse. And joy comes when you can look forward and know in your heart, "Whatever comes and whatever we face, we will face it together by God's grace."

Don't expect love to always be fun and romantic. Remember that true love takes hard work and a humble heart. And true love is what matters most.

What next?

Let love cost you today; choose to sacrifice for your loved one. Make a plan and then act.

May I pray for you?

God, your love for us cost you immeasurably. We broke your heart, yet you gave us your son. Help us become people who will work hard for what matters. And nothing matters more than love. Amen.

DAY 90: BETWEEN THE CROSS AND EASTER

"I am the resurrection and the life. The one who believes in me will live, even though they die; and whoever lives by believing in me will never die" John 11:25-26.

Jesus's disciples had a horrible day the Saturday after the crucifixion. In hindsight, we know it as the period between the cross and Easter, but they didn't see it that way.

Their teacher, rabbi, Lord, and closest friend lay dead in a cold tomb, along with their dream of a Messianic-led rebirth of Israel.

The disciples feared for their lives as they cowered in an upper room somewhere in the city of Jerusalem. Overnight they had become religious outcasts among the very people who once sang the praises of Jesus and his motley crew.

Yesterday, the Friday of his crucifixion, they ran, they denied, they watched from a distance in horror, and they wept in agony. Today, they lived in shock, in dread, and in dark corners of deafening silence. Remember, they did not understand the promise of the resurrection.

Not yet.

In those moments, their limited perspective didn't allow for hope in a better tomorrow.

I wonder how many of you are in a similar place? Something, or maybe even someone, has died. You've lost a dream, a relationship, a job or a friend, and you're an exhausted, emotional and physical wreck. You can't even think about the future.

If that's you, please listen to these words: God knows where you've been, where you're at, and where he will take you. He understands the crushing anguish of the cross, but he also knows (far better than you do) tomorrow is a brand new day.

So hold on. Stay true. Don't despair. Sunday is just around the corner.

What next?
If you're struggling today, find some friends who can walk with you through your trials, and together take them to the Lord.

May I pray for you?
God, sometimes the misery of yesterday and the emptiness of today steal our joy and hope for tomorrow. Sometimes numbness covers our hearts, minds, and souls like a dense winter fog and we can't even think about the future. Help us trust and follow you even when life is bleak. Wrap your arms around us, Lord, and comfort us amidst our pain. Amen.

ACKNOWLEDGEMENTS

I am so grateful for the writing and editing skills of Lindsay Branting and her incredible support on this project. Lindsay is a gifted copyeditor and writer in her own right as well as a special family friend.

My amazing daughter, Jessica Harris, once again provided her editing and proofing expertise with this book. Thank you for your labor of love.

I also want to thank the church I have the pleasure of pastoring and my fellow Eastpointers. Your encouragement and love inspires me to serve with joy. You are loved.

Perfectly Imperfect ~ A Devotional

ABOUT THE AUTHORS

Kurt W. Bubna published his first book, *Epic Grace ~ Chronicles of a Recovering Idiot*, with Tyndale in 2013. His second book, *Mr. & Mrs.: How to Thrive in a Perfectly Imperfect Marriage* was released in October or 2014. He is an active blogger (kurtbubna.com), and the Sr. Pastor of Eastpoint Church in Spokane Valley, Washington. He and his wife Laura have been married for nearly forty years and have four grown children and five grandchildren.

Lindsay Branting is a freelance writer and copyeditor. She spends most of her waking hours huddled over a computer screen working on her own or other's written masterpieces. Married with two great kids, she resides in Spokane, Washington. This is her first co-authored work.

www.ingramcontent.com/pod-product-compliance
Lightning Source LLC
Chambersburg PA
CBHW060010050426
42448CB00012B/2689